purge

PURGE

created and performed
by Brian Lobel

OBERON BOOKS
LONDON

WWW.OBERONBOOKS.COM

First published in 2016 by Oberon Books Ltd
521 Caledonian Road, London N7 9RH
Tel: +44 (0) 20 7607 3637 / Fax: +44 (0) 20 7607 3629
e-mail: info@oberonbooks.com
www.oberonbooks.com

PB ISBN: 9781783193295
E ISBN: 9781783193301

Cover image by Mamoru Iriguchi
Cover design and text layout by Konstantinos Vasdekis

Printed and bound by 4edge Limited, Essex, UK.
eBook conversion by Lapiz Digital Services, India.

Visit www.oberonbooks.com to read more about all our books
and to buy them. You will also find features, author interviews and
news of any author events, and you can sign up for e-newsletters
so that you're always first to hear about our new releases.

CONTENTS

Acknowledgements

Purge was, essentially, a collaborative performance that I made with 1400 Facebook friends. Without their humor, their consent, their engagement and even their criticism, this quite-straightforward concept I had for a performance would never had felt so far-reaching and significant. While I was overwhelmed by the email maintenance caused by *Purge*, I was also humbled by the intelligence, candor and depth of this community that feels anything but virtual.

I would also like to thank the audiences who have come to *Purge* since it became a stage show in 2013. The nature of creating an interactive performance, which is more like an hour spent with friends then a formal stage show, means that all of the audience interactions, stories told, and people deleted have made the script what it is. I hope – if you were an audience member – you'll find the work indicative of what you saw, and inclusive of the energy and heart that you brought to the theater each night.

I would like to thank the programmers, producers and venue managers who supported the work at various stages – from commissioners motiroti, to café owners throughout London who hosted *Purge,* to presenting partners like ANTI Contemporary Art Festival, Vooruit, Rich Mix and others who provided space for the work at its early stages – to current presenters who continue to bring the work to many throughout the world, allowing the story of *Purge* to continue to grow. I am thankful for the hard work and dedication of Charlene Lim, Tracy Gentles and Hannah Slimmon, the first producer who worked with me to transform *Purge* from installation to stage work. I am also thankful to Arts Council England who supported this development.

I am also deeply indebted to those who lent their talents to make *Purge* happen: namely, Chipp Jansen (computer design), Mamoru Iriguchi (graphic design), and Season

Acknowledgements

Butler, who steadfastly supported *Purge* for all 50 hours of its installation, and whose friendship is something I treasure. I am also thankful to Priya Agrawal and the family of Grant R. Folland, who have been so supportive in my endeavors and continue to support *Purge* and the work I have made about Grant's passing. I hope I honor them and him through my performances.

Purge may have forced me to reconsider the definition of friendship in the era of social networking, and this may be something which continues to change over time. But after talking and talking and talking about what makes a friend I know one thing firmly: friendship is not defined by the words you say, but by the smile that you get when you hear their name or see their face. Those audience members who sat with me in the installation could see it instantly... a warm smile, a relaxation in my face, some genuine light behind my eyes. It never took more than a second or two to tell. And I am thankful – as cheesy as it may sound – for all those who make me smile.

Purge/Puhdistus Installation in Kuopio, Finland
Photo by Pekka Mäkinen
Courtesy of ANTI Contemporary Art Festival, 2011

Purge Installation in London, UK
Photo by Sophie Allen, 2011

Purge Installation in London, UK
Photo by Sophie Allen, 2011

Brian and Season mark the final minute of
Purge/Puhdistus Installation, Kuopio, Finland
Photo by Pekka Mäkinen
Courtesy of ANTI Contemporary Art Festival, 2011

Chronology and Performance History

2011

11 June, *Purge* announced via Facebook. 68 Facebook friends pre-emptively deleted themselves within one hour

11-15 June, 800+ emailed, messaged and texted responses received

7-10 July, performance of *Purge*, the installation, across four different London venues: Jasmine Kitchen (Tower Hill), Brick Box (Brixton), First Out (Central London), Off-Broadway (Hackney)

10 July, 'Former Friends of Brian Lobel' Group appears on Facebook, founded by deleted (and later re-added) friend Margherita Laera

27 September-1 October, performance of *Purge/Puhdistus*, the installation, in the foyer of the Kuopio Academy of Design, for ANTI Contemporary Art Festival

Purge/Puhdistus wins 'Kiltein/Kindest' and 'Idioottimaisin/Most Idiotic' Performance at ANTI Children's Choice Awards

2012

Talk about *Purge* to University of Leeds – New Stages Festival

Purge wins the Digital Writing Award, given by Edge Hill University, North West Playwrights and Capital Theatre Festival

Work-in-progress of *Purge* presented at Rich Mix, London
Developed with support from Arts Council England
Produced by Hannah Kerr
Featured co-performer Dan Watson (a Facebook friend deleted in the original installation)

Work-in-progress of *Purge* presented at SummerWorks Performance Festival – Toronto

Purge at Small Projects – Tromsø[1]

Purge at Rose Theatre, Edge Hill University – Ormskirk
Featured co-performer Caroline Molloy (a Facebook friend
deleted in the original installation)

Purge at Vooruit – Ghent
Accompanied by *Purge* installation recreated by Isabelle Bats
for the Fail Conference (first half of her friends)

2013

Purge at Beursschouwburg – Brussels
Accompanied by *Purge* installation recreated by Isabelle Bats
for Private Investigations Festival (second half of her friends)

Purge at Showroom, University of Chichester – Chichester

Purge at Camden People's Theatre – London

Purge at Contact for Flying Solo Festival – Manchester

Purge at Maison des arts de Créteil (MAC) for EXIT Festival
– Paris
Accompanied by *Purge* installation recreated by Chrissie Dante[2]
Purge translated into French by Chloé Déchery

Purge at Cambridge Junction – Cambridge
Featured co-performer Eirini Kartsaki (a Facebook friend
deleted in the original installation)

---

[1] The show never really had a premiere I just stopped calling it a
Work-in-Progress. While the show no longer changes significantly
in its format, the details change according to what has actually
happened in my life/the subjects' lives. I also believe I have
gotten better at performing *Purge*, so that's changed.

[2] Those individuals who use a pseudonym for their engagement
with social networking performed the installation as this identity
and were credited under their Facebook name.

Brian Lobel

Purge at Latitude Festival – Southwold
A performance about technology performed without technology

Purge at Santarcangelo Festival Dei Teatri – Santarcangelo
Accompanied by *Purge* installation recreated by Alba von Von
Purge translated into Italian by Michelle Davis

Purge at PSi (Performance Studies International) at Stanford
University – Palo Alto

Purge at Battersea Arts Centre – London

Purge at Forest Fringe, Out of the Blue Drill Hall – Edinburgh

Purge at JW3 – London

Purge at Canada Water Culture Space – London

2014

Purge at Kakiseni – Kuala Lumpur
Accompanied by a live twitter-pretation by Niki Cheong

Purge at Infecting the City Festival – Cape Town
Accompanied by *Purge* installation recreated by
Amy Jephta

Purge at Tojo Theatre and Turnhalle for AUAWIRLEBEN
Theaterfestival – Bern
Accompanied by *Purge* installation recreated by
Diego Häberli

Purge at Brighton Dome Studio for Brighton Festival
– Brighton

Purge at New Wolsey Theatre for PULSE14 – Ipswich

Purge at Forest Fringe Microfestival, Abrons Arts Centre
– New York City

2015

Purge at Live Art Bistro (LAB) – Leeds

Purge at Off-Center for Fusebox Festival – Austin
Accompanied by *Purge* installation recreated by Jeff Mills
and Kymberlie Quong Charles[3/4]

2016

Purge at Freedom Park, part of the Lagos Theatre Festival
– Lagos
Featured co-performers Gideon Okeke and Marcy Dolapo Oni[5]

Purge at Old Folks Association – Auckland

Purge at NUS Arts Festival – Singapore

Purge at Malthouse Theatre, part of the Melbourne
International Comedy Festival – Melbourne

Purge at Colchester Arts Centre – Colchester

Purge at Southbank Centre, part of the Festival of Love
– London

---

[3] In May 2015, Facebook updated its API to limit the access of
Facebook Apps to a user's friend network. This was due to critiques
of exposing user's information to third-party apps. This new technical
limitation broke the Purge App's main functionality of accessing
a user's friend list and as such, the app, and the performance
installation using the app, were retired.

[4] A footnote to the previous footnote: the previous footnote's
app jargon was, of course, courtesy of technical designer Chipp
Jansen.

[5] As of July 2016 – when this book when to print – homosexuality is
an imprisonable offense in Nigeria, despite there being a thriving,
if still unseen, LGBTQ community in Lagos. I made the – at some
times heartbreaking – decision to edit *Purge*, deleting much of
the gay content, and calling Grant 'my best friend'. This was not
an alteration requested by the festival, but my own choice. The
change from 'first boyfriend' to 'best friend' fooled absolutely no
one, and that was fine for me. The co-performers – both soap
stars and tv personalities – were incorporated into the work by
acting the responses from my friends. They were wonderful, and
definitely proved that I am not, never have been, never will be,
a good actor.

Introduction

Grief, to me, is walking into a room of strangers, colleagues or even friends, and instantly thinking about not only whom I would trade, but how actively I would participate in their death in hopes of bringing Grant back to life. Back to life forever? For five minutes? For a day? For long enough for a hug? A kiss? For long enough for one of our 25-year-old, stumbling sexual encounters that characterized our relationship so so many years ago? So, for like, 15 minutes?

I know that I am grieving when my calculations are complicated, mathematically speaking. Would I kill someone with my own hands if I could have a day with him? Would I sit by and watch someone else die if it meant I could hear his voice? And would his voice say something I've heard before or something new? Would he be able to provide an answer to one of the many questions I have, questions that are such a hallmark of relationships (friendships, families and beyond) that are ended in an instant?

Grant R. Folland was, and still is, my favorite person in the world. He was a man who thought critically, wrote beautifully, and gave generously to his friends and family. He was also my first love, first boyfriend (although I'm not sure if we ever used that word with each other) and the person for whom I would happily trade any one of you reading this. Sorry. While I no longer (or at least not so often) calculate the aforementioned murderous equations in my mind, I know that there is very little I wouldn't do to feel his embrace or hear his voice again.

At the time of his death in 2010 – when Grant died instantly while snowmobiling – I can write without pause that we were best friends. Perhaps we would have even rekindled our romantic relationship in the future... such delusional theoretical predictions are the stuff of grief and uncertainty. Even if we did ever get back together in the future... we would have definitely broken up again, maybe even broken up as friends... ours was a love and a friendship which fitted so perfectly in some ways and so difficultly in others.

I need to start a book about *Purge* with a conversation about grief, because I don't want anyone to think that *Purge* was about social media and/or technology. Maybe it is a bit about social media, but only insomuch as contemporary beings discuss, share, enact and (potentially, hopefully) heal from grief on, via and through social media. It is, for many aside from a few stalwart technophobes, the stuff of life itself. I am not precious enough about the 'live', the 'corporeal' or the 'tactile' to pretend that these worlds are anything too separate from the 'digital' and the 'connected'. But no, *Purge* is not about social media. It's about grief, and loss, and disconnection. And – above all else – I hope it is about Grant.

Perhaps the reason why this story is told via social media is because Grant and I lived our lives and our relationship through social media and internet communication. From our first Friendster messages, to obtaining celebrity gmail accounts for each other (Midori.Ito and India.Arie remain personal favorites), to constant messaging during the day, to stalking each other (and our current flings/boyfriends/partners), to leaving and answering Craigslist Missed Connections for each other... electronic communication suited us just fine. And never once did I feel like the body or physical presence was missing – until, of course, he was gone, and the emails and messages, bereft of their physical referent, floated like untethered balloons. I floated with them.

This introduction digresses and rambles, my apologies. BUT HE WAS FUCKING AWESOME AND I WISH YOU KNEW HIM.

I don't want you to think that I began this Introduction with a long, emotional outpouring about Grant in hopes of silencing the critiques that many people had of *Purge*. Discussion of death and trauma is often used to silence, to bully people into acquiescing (a reality I know all too well from my time studying and working with cancer patients) and I don't want to replicate that silencing here. And I hope that you'll feel as though, after reading this book, that I've given fair and respectful space to those people who were emotionally, politically or intellectually unhappy about *Purge*. But I did need you to know that this was a performance made from a space of grief, and explain what I mean when I talk about losing someone, and the negatives and (perhaps, possibly) the positives that come with.

I had many friends that knew me both in person and via social networking, and knew I was grieving very seriously over Grant's death, and of these people, a number got in touch, worried about *Purge* and my mental health. For many, *Purge* represented quite a violent cleaning – of my personal life, of my relationships, of the 'junk' of contemporary social networking – that felt reminiscent of a person getting their affairs in order, or giving things away, before a suicide. But I was not suicidal, I was just really sad, and unaware of how dangerous a project like *Purge* might be for my mental health.

In the winter of 2011, I began applying for spaces to make/ show *Purge* as the second piece of a trilogy called *Mourning Glory* (about the impact and particulars of Grant's death) and was successful with London-based arts organization motiroti and with ANTI Festival of Contemporary Art in Kuopio, Finland. Although I had only intended to do *Purge* one time – as one, 25-hour installation felt like long enough – they were both accepted within a week of each other, and so I decided to do a London-based *Purge* in July, and Kuopio-based *Purge in* October. The final day of *Purge* took place on both my 30th Birthday (October 1st, 2011) and on Yom Kippur, the Jewish Day of Atonement. It all seemed so terribly, cosmically, in synch.

I began workshopping *Purge*, designing the technology (made by genius artist-computer whizz Chipp Jansen), commissioning the imagery (made by the brilliant artist-designer Mamoru Iriguchi), and was instantly overwhelmed with fears and questions about legality. Was I committing libel by livestreaming a discussion of my social network? Was I going against Facebook's Terms & Conditions? And, most importantly, was I being ethical in my artistic pursuits? After the initial applications to do *Purge*, reality set in: a lot of people, by the end of this process, might hate me.

And they did. Hate me. When I announced *Purge* in June 2011, within one hour I was deleted by 68 people. Within three days, I had received over 800 emails, Facebook messages and comments. Many were engaged and excited by the project – which is overwhelming in its own way, as even positive emails demand some kind of immediate response or engagement – others were very, very angry. What you hear in the show itself is but the tip of the iceberg, the most cohesive of the arguments against and anger from *Purge*, but there were plenty. While I was bruised by the angry comments left on my Facebook Wall – 'Stupid and a waste of time.' – 'Who the fuck is this person!' for me it was worst when people silently deleted me. I took stock of some of the people who deleted me pre-emptively: my mentor, my favorite one-night stand in Chicago, a DJ I loved in Los Angeles, an activist I respected from South Africa... and they were gone. And even though I had caused them to do it – and, hell, I had even recommended that they Delete me if they didn't want to be part of the show – I was really shaken.

But if 20% of the responses were nasty and offended, 80% were engaged and enthusiastic. Suddenly I was in touch with people from my past, my present, my distant past and even my future. I became fascinated with social networking and how, on the lead up to my 30th birthday, talking about each of my 1400 Facebook friends for one minute became a strange and really long autobiographical performance. Because the show went in alphabetical order, it was completely random – one minute I spoke about my cancer nurse, the next about a camper that I had in my bunk. One minute I was talking about a porn star that came to the club I worked at in London, the next minute, a religious woman who I volunteered with in Albany, New York.

For me, the close proximity of all these histories and backgrounds are what make social networking so overwhelming and stress-inducing: your bigoted cousin's rant is next to your ex's wedding photos, next to cat videos by your boss (who shouldn't be posting cat videos during work hours) and worthy folk asking for money for yet another worthy cause. *Purge*, with its one-minute, one-person structure, became a physical manifestation of the overwhelming energy often necessary to stay on top of social networking and contemporary media. While the 25-hour installation (5-7 hours, 4-5 days in a row) was fun and funny to watch (some reported watching the livestream for up to six hours at a time) it was also horrifying: my body became exhausted, voice hoarse, brain fried. I was so thankful to Season Butler, one of my closest friends, who worked with me throughout both installations – she knew when it was over that I just needed to sleep, or drink, or (ideally) drink drink drink, and then sleep. Season's work in the space – coordinating audiences, running the livestream, keeping me watered and caffeinated – was invaluable, and she performed the work with care and kindness.

I will not be the first artist to have destroyed all their possessions (I was particularly inspired by Michael Landy's *Break Down*, 2001) or ended relationships through performance (Marina Abramovic and Ulay's *The Lovers*, 1988), but I think I may have been the first to do this via social media. This may be a function of the relative newness of social networking, or that the form's presence in a time of liquid modernity (a term coined by sociologist Zygmunt Bauman to describe the ambivalence and fluidity of contemporary identities) may make this a place where the threat of a disconnection is not so serious, as relationships are now considered temporary and added/subtracted with the oh-so-easy work of a click one way or another.

But *Purge* may also be one of the first of its kind because, it seems to me, that most people still currently view more networks, more connections, more friends, more followers as an uncomplicatedly good thing. Although many are well aware of the pitfalls associated with overconsumption, we are less critical of what all the links, views and friends might be doing. 'Going viral' is a ridiculous way to talk about something being awesome and popular (ask anyone living inside an epidemic) and yet, most who engage with social media and networking still feel it is the goal. But what of the small, the impactless, the local. Is the opposite of going viral, staying healthy? I like to think of *Purge* as something which helps us stay healthy. The title is meant to invoke both the rapid, almost violent cleaning which ends in heaps and heaps of trash bags, or the vomit which finally clears out the system after a big night of drinking or the final vomit in a stomach flu. It hurts (both physically and emotionally), it's gross, it's unpleasant, and it's totally necessary. And afterwards, after that minute or two of shakiness and unease, you feel... better.

It should be noted that *Purge* was created before Facebook introduced the Unfollow Button, before it had such a sophisticated and business-focused algorithm and before people had quite strict policies about who should and should not be one's Facebook friends. The social networking world of 2011 feels positively naïve compared to today, where nearly everyone has a totally objective, personal Facebook policy (which is most often deployed in moments of conflict when people berate those who have encroached on their digital safe space) and keeping – but unfollowing – is the norm. While I wouldn't be so bold as to say that Facebook's Unfollow option was a direct result of the press received during *Purge*, I do find the evolution from de-friending to un-following to be but another piece of evidence of how more and more connections are privileged, and also evidence of how far people are willing to go to still be considered nice.

Purge was not nice, and I deeply regret that *Purge* caused such sadness or discomfort in a number of people. The fact that I was grieving is an excuse but not good enough as an excuse. And besides, none of the materials which Facebook friends saw at the time were related to grief, so even if they would be compassionate about it, they wouldn't have known the work's origin. But for so many of the relationships that changed via *Purge,* nearly all of them changed for the better. Instead of friendships which lay dormant – determined by a Friend Request and Acceptance years ago, *Purge* ensured that each friendship was rigorously tested and considered. And though the email maintenance was beyond anything I had experienced, it was really nice to hear from so many people, to peek in on their lives, to share with them – even briefly – as once we had. The greatest problem with social networking is not that friendships become digitized and simple, but that they become unused and taken for granted. There they are, in that digital space, just where you left them. This isn't good enough for a friendship – a real friendship must be activated, wrestled with and celebrated. Or I guess that's how I currently define it, a definition which will, of course (as I learned from *Purge*) be different from everyone else and perhaps even to myself in the future.

It is this ambiguity, this lack of definition, this lack of certainty, which brings me back, heartbreakingly, to Grant, to our relationship, and to his death. After years of making work about cancer and with cancer patients, I thought I knew everything there was to know about loss, everything about the style which befit serious subjects, and how to speak, theatrically and artistically, about struggle and death, but I was wrong. And suddenly, six months after his death, finally coming out of the thick haze of mourning, I found myself needing to reconsider all the truths that I had known about creating

Introduction

work about the body, vulnerability and mortality. Shortly after, I found myself tentatively sharing the idea of *Purge* with my bereavement counselor at St. Joseph's Hospice. Although she thought it was a terrible idea and did actually try to convince me out of doing it, when I saw the horror on her face (scared for my own mental and emotional well-being) I knew I was on to something.

Perhaps a performance about grief needs to feature something that makes people angry and makes people uncomfortable. Maybe a performance about grief needs to feature real life stakes, real sadness, real anger, real disruption. My desire to tell a story about Grant – with beautiful language, and intelligently constructed metaphor – was dampened by my knowledge that no matter how good a writer I was, no words would capture his brilliance. And if I really did tell you how amazing he was, you wouldn't believe it. So instead, I decided to create a performance that fried my brain, overwhelmed my email, and pissed a lot of people off. As a tribute to Grant. And I certainly hope he'd be fine with that.

Bibliography

Abramović, Marina and Ulay (1989) *The Lovers,*
Amsterdam: Stedelijk Museum

Bauman, Zygmunt (2003) *Liquid Love,*
Cambridge: Polity Press

Landy, Michael (2008) *Everything Must Go!,*
London: Ridinghouse

Response from Season Butler, *Purge* Associate Artist

A somewhat hasty assumption exists that the internet has made us all superficial, narcissistic, silly enough to mistake social media interaction for *genuine* friendship: encounters accompanied by smells and stains from toothpaste drool and all the other peccadillos of embodiedness. As if we now replace intimacy with an 'Add Friend' click, and break-ups have become as simple as hitting 'Delete.' In my experience, for better or worse, we're not there yet.

The responses to Brian's pre-*Purge* form letter go some small way to supporting this point. Because of a personal relationship, 1,342 people found that, for sixty seconds, one of their friendships would be converted into a metaphor. This provocation inspired responses from the moralistic to the flirtatious, the appalled to the admiring.

I take the view that, in art, everything is fair game. (Of course, the few occasions when I've recognised myself in someone else's work tested this principle. A favourable nod in a show by Project O sent my ego soaring; my appearance in a short story by one of my creative writing students called up a plaintive whine of '*but...but...but...*' which I laboured to keep inside.)

Brian's body of work has a deep grounding in autobiography. He lays his geekiness bare in *Hold My Hand and We're Halfway There*, inviting an audience to be together in the ecstasy of dancing alone to guilty-pleasure video viewing, letting us all be our most unabashed, unembarrassed in how embarrassing we really are. *BALL, An Appreciation*, and other work arising from his experience with cancer come from very particular experiences and memories but which have an astounding reach, shrewdly evoking insights into something as basic, and as universal, as having a body – and having a body that changes.

But in *Purge*, he was using his life *in relation to* other people. What he valued in them. What, for him, made the relationship worthwhile. Any of us might be expunged, surf a wave of performance art bile out of his friend list and get flushed away.

Brian Lobel has always been the person I know (like, really know, IRL) with the most Facebook 'friends.' He also happens to be the person I know with the most friends, making connections everywhere he goes with jaw-dropping ease. To me, his Facebook friend list never seemed like a cynical mailing list cobbled together for bald utility, nor even the revenge of a gregarious adult who'd once been a dweeby kid, but a mass of genuine links irrespective of the vintage of the relationship. I never worried that he'd treat his friendships exploitatively, but maybe that's because I know him, y'know, IRL.

This was the point that emerged for me as I watched Brian's minute-long descriptions of his friends and their relationships. The bilious violence implied by the show's title, the recklessness of the random panel, the gladiatorial ring of the thumbs-up/thumbs-down verdicts summoning the terminal deletion of a person from a place where they once existed but wouldn't any more: under all of this, the show's feisty surface concealed something almost heroic. Far from feeding his friendships to the lions, he was their champion. Each time the clock reset and started ticking down, Brian launched a valiant defence, breathless to recount every detail, persuading by remembering.

(Here I'm reminded of the warning window that pops-up when I try to close a document too hastily: *Your changes will be lost if you don't save them...*)

There was always something more to *Purge* than simply risking people's feelings or testing their good-will for the dramatic potential that high stakes provide. After all, the friend who was rendered the most vulnerable here was Brian. The choice to keep or delete was a test of *his* friendship, *his* ability to put into words why each connection was valuable, why each person was irreplaceable. On the few occasions when a 'friendship' really justified the scare quotes, Brian was honest about that, too.

During the first 25-hour performance installation, there was only one person out of all the hundreds about whom he could remember nothing. Deleted.

23

Purge strongly connotes catharsis, maybe even a restorative one – violent in its throes, and then we feel better having released something, let something go. It is, after all, a show rooted in grief. But *Purge* is also about remembering, using social media as an archive. Like an archive, our 'friend' list can be an unseen, seldom-opened receptacle gathering dust in the corners of our online profiles. To make *Purge*, Brian had to fling his open, not taking anyone (friend or 'friend') for granted, realising that to do so would be an easy and profound mistake.

Considering the formal elements of repetition and duration draws a reading of *Purge* beyond its hundreds of biographical vignettes and asks us to think of the piece as a process. Like Sophie Calle, Brian deploys the repetition of a regulated framework over what feels like a deeply protracted duration to encounter truths that can feel senselessly cruel, over and over again.

Purge is a confrontation with loss, an affirmation of friendship and an acknowledgement of the precarious nature of our ties to other people. If these relationships hadn't meant anything, if they were just the superficial yield of networking events, connections to be exploited as the social capital of the selfie generation, *Purge* would not have been such compelling viewing. Nebulous forces like fate were materialised in the judgements of a panel of Finnish school kids hearing Brian's defences in translation, or the jilted lover with an axe to grind against an ex (okay, that was me). The piece is interesting not because it treats friendships as disposable, but because it shows that the durability of a friendship can be an act of will in the face of life's endless fickleness. Grounded as it is in the violence of loss, *Purge* reminds us to consider what we value in the people we know, and to let go of the ties we no longer need with gratitude and levity and grace.

With love,
Season Butler
London, 2016

Season Butler and the *Purge/Puhdistus* livestream,
Kuopio, Finland
Photo by Pekka Mäkinen
Courtesy of ANTI Contemporary Art Festival, 2011

A Note about Performing *Purge*

The inclusion of the Amateur Performing Rights disclaimer, which comes along with the plays published by Oberon, inspires a unique reflection. A few years ago, I wrote a note alongside my script of *BALL & Other Funny Stories About Cancer* that it felt weird to have people perform texts that were written about my real body, my real scars and my real history with cancer. Similarly, it feels weird to think of people performing texts written about my real relationships, and from my real friends. But, as Gabriela wrote so eloquently in her response to *Purge* (pg 44), 'I should think of your performing self, no matter how confessional, as being something of an artificial persona, and that my name, therefore, was kind of a fiction, too.' The texts here came from real people in my life, but of course they are – to the overwhelming majority of readers – strangers. And in this way, perhaps it's not that weird for you to perform *Purge* as a fictional work.

I would challenge you, though, instead of performing the script as you read here, to think of the text of the show as an example: an open document you can and should fill with your own experience. Instead of reading about how I did *Purge*, you should inform your social network that you'll be deleting people via public vote, wait for their responses, and then build a show of your own. I promise that – as you'll read from the responses of my friends – when prompted, people will contribute absolutely magnificent things. And these contributions will not be the words of fictional strangers to you, they will be friends – or at least Facebook friends – and you'll hopefully have something to say about each one. And I promise this will make for an even better show for you to perform.

Purge at The Showroom, Chichester

Photos by Aaron Reeves

Purge

(As the audience arrives, Brian is already on stage, sitting at a computer, wearing a t-shirt reading I Like You and updating his Facebook status, which continues for up to ten minutes.[6] 'Together in Electric Dreams' (Philip Oakey and Giorgio Moroder, 1984) plays, as does Dionne Warwick's cover of 'That's What Friends Are For', 1985. If more time is needed, Brian – controlling the music from the laptop he is typing from – opens up iTunes and rewinds the track of 'That's What Friends Are For'. Audience members are encouraged, via the status update, to sing along. When 'Nothing Compares 2 U' (Prince, 1993) begins, Brian opens his list of Facebook Friends and begins scrolling down. As the chorus plays, Brian un-friends one Facebook contact. Brian logs out of his account, fades the music on the iTunes, and the show begins.)[7]

1:00 Countdown (featuring a digital alarm at :00)

I was directing a play — a very bad play — that was my first professional directing gig in Chicago. Actually they were two short plays: *The Gunslinger*, by a friend, Kalena Dickerson, that was actually really good, and then *The Fall of an Acorn*, or something like that, by Jesse something. I don't remember, and together they were not very good, horrible actually, but many of the actors remain my Facebook friends today. It was one of those gigs where I direct the show, make the costumes, hang the lights, build the set. Although with the set-building my friend Marc, who was the playwright Kalena's boyfriend, was doing the construction, and I was doing the decorations and embellishments.

---

[6] For example status updates, see page 54.

[7] A note on the fonts in the script. ***Bolded texts*** are the writing on the projection. *Italicised texts* written in third person are stage directions. **Klavika Bold texts** are verbatim texts either sent by or received by myself. All other texts are scripted, but often susceptible to embellishments, abbreviations, and improvisation. I have tried to capture these interludes and discussion as close as possible to an average night's performance.

Purge

The theater — Breadline Theater, now defunct — was split into two buildings. One was the main house, where the street address to the theater was, and the other a studio in the building behind — in a building filled with art studios — where the show would actually happen. It was really a disgusting little place, incredibly run-down, asbestos-filled. Marc was working in the front room, while I was in the back. The studio space was weird at night — people would work late, work loudly, or it would be completely silent. It was very unpredictable. I didn't mind working alone but I didn't love it either...

Message received by over 300 people via Facebook messenger.

Dear Friend, or, rather, Dear Former Friend

This email is to notify you that we are no longer Facebook friends. As part of my performance Purge, I asked strangers to vote on whether to keep or delete you from my list of friends. I described and defended our relationship for one minute, but apparently, what I said was not good enough. They have decided to DELETE.

I miss you already.

There are a few choices moving forward:
1) We could never speak again, if you never want to speak again.
2) We could become Facebook friends again in the future, either now (if you choose to re-friend me) or sometime down the line.
3) We could create a different path for our relationship in this world, to be determined by you, and, I guess, by me.

Thank you for your friendship, past, present and (I hope) future.

warmly, Brian

Grant

After Grant died, I began compiling all of our emails into a single document, an attempt somehow to archive our tumultuous relationship from first loves, to first heartbreaks, to something that was difficult to describe in words.

But our very first electronic exchange was not via email, but rather on Friendster message. Friendster was a pre-Facebook/Myspace social networking tool that whet my appetite for online social networking. In 2003, Friendster rejected a $30million buyout offer from Google, which began a slow spiral to irrelevance for users in the USA (where I was living at the time) and users in the UK and Europe. I tried to hold on to my Friendsters but by 2006, most of my friends had migrated to Facebook or Myspace.

Grant and I only shared two exchanges on Friendster, each heavy with geek-love-wordplay that were intended to impress the other with our wit and to hint at our romantic interest. He was a magnificent writer. When I went to find those first Friendster messages, I noticed something: 'Add As Friend', it said. Add As Friend. Why would I have to Add Grant as a Friend? We were friends. Or were we?

This was the moment that I realized that Grant had de-friended me on Friendster. We had become Myspace Friends and Facebook Friends, and when he died we were still best friends – but apparently, at some point along the way, in 2006, Grant had decided that we shouldn't be friends. Perhaps it was too hard post-break-up. Perhaps he just didn't like me very much at the time. I hadn't been on Friendster in over four years, but the severing of this electronic relationship left me bereft. And searching for answers.

Purge Logo

You've wanted to do it for so long. Every time you see their face in this digital space, you cringe, you sweat, you lose a little piece of yourself. But would they notice? Do you care if they would? Why did you ever have this connection in the first place? Why are we here, together?

At this point in PURGE, audience members shout out the kinds of people they would delete from their social network right now, if they could

(The lights in the audience turn on quickly, and the audience will remain well-lit until the end of the show. Audience members shout out the kinds of people they want to delete, while Brian facilitates their participation.) [8]

1:00 Countdown (featuring a digital alarm at :00)

In 2005, I was directing a play — a very bad play. Marc was working in the front room, while I was in the back. The studio space was weird at night — people would work late, work loudly, or it would be completely silent. It was very unpredictable.

On this day in particular, I was talking on the phone to Grant, my new favorite person in the entire world. I had met Grant a few weeks earlier at a performance that I gave in his home town — East Lansing, Michigan, a 5-hour drive from Chicago — and was out of my mind with excitement at how he was going to be moving to the city in September to start law school. We emailed the most beautiful emails to each other three times a day, and talked on the phone the rest of the time. He was witty, dark-humoured and described how he felt through the lyrics of Prince songs... not romantic songs like

---

[8] Frequently-named people who others wish to delete: bigoted relatives, bullies from school, work colleagues/bosses, those with consistent profile pictures of baby/wedding, humble braggers, religious relatives, those who incessantly invite others to play Candy Crush, Farmville, etc., and 'monitoring spirits' – a term introduced by audiences in Nigeria to describe those who watch your status, but don't comment or add to the online community.

Stevie Wonder songs, but nasty, sexy Prince songs. Although he hated talking on the phone, I had convinced him to speak nightly and he did so begrudgingly. It's about 2am Chicago time, 3am Michigan time, and Grant was worried about how late I was working.

'It's no problem, the show opens in a few days,' I said, 'but what I'm really concerned about is the shrieking studio neighbor. If you don't hear from me in the morning, I've probably been axe-murdered.' The banging continued to happen in the studio next door to mine, and while I hated not knowing exactly what that horrifying noise was, I mostly just thought it was someone wielding a hard-to-manage sledgehammer or something art-creation related.

Email to 1342 Facebook friends

Dear Friend:

This is, purposefully, a form letter.

I am writing because a new show that I'm doing, entitled Purge, will involve you and the rest of my Facebook community. I will be inviting strangers to decide whether to keep or delete each of my individual Facebook friends. Here's how it will work:

1) The show will run 6 hours each day, with 5 minute breaks each hour.

2) Going in alphabetical order, each Facebook friend will be considered for one minute. Inside this minute, I will Describe my relationship with each person, Defend having them as a Facebook friend, and then it will be Decided whether to keep that relationship or not. I am well aware that one minute is a woefully short amount of time, but it will allow me to perform the work and talk about each friend equally. It will also prove an exhausting experience, and allow me to speak most from the gut where, I believe, friendships may be best evaluated.

3) Three audience members at a time will vote to KEEP or DELETE. If deleted, I will send the contact a form letter (much like this) describing that three strangers, based on the information I discussed with them, have decided that we should not be friends, or that we should not be Facebook friends.

4) Because the audience members on the three-person panel will change constantly, each new panel will bring to the voting its own ethics about who should be one's Facebook friend and who should not be.

5) The atmosphere will be a combination of casual coffee with friends and high-octane game show.

I will be making a few assurances to you, my friends, my Facebook friends, and all those in between.

1) I will not say anything untrue.

2) I will have a livestream of the event available to be watched. This will evidence that I am not acting in bad faith, lying, or doing anything otherwise unethical.

3) I will discuss each person for only 60 seconds.

4) If you are still uncomfortable with Purge, but still want to be my Facebook friend, email me, we can find a way for you to be comfortable.

As I see it, you have a few options for how to proceed from here.

1) Delete me pre-emptively.

2) Put me on 'limited profile' so that your information will not be seen by others.

3) Tell me the story you'd like me to relate about us to the audience in hopes of keeping our friendship, even electronically, alive.

The project is not an endorsement of Facebook or its policies, nor is it a critique of them. It's just that Facebook is the social networking site that I use the most at this time.

Thank you so much for reading. I look forward to hearing from you. I don't mean to be so formal in an email – especially because I bet we have a very playful, meaningful friendship – but I wanted to get everyone this information.

warmly, Brian

Responses were swift.

> **KEVIN**
> **So even though I know you and have been friends with you for a while, you're going to have strangers make a decision about whether we should remain Facebook friends as some... performance piece? As you suggested, I have deleted you pre-emptively.**

It's probably good that Kevin deleted me as, during my one minute, all I'd have to say was that we used to live in the same apartment complex and have sex when his boyfriend was away on work trips.

But, after responses like Kevin's and 68 people deleting me in the hour after that email was sent, there were many wonderful, brilliant and funny responses as well. In fact, the overwhelming majority were engaged, excited and nervous.

Let's see if your opinions match the judging panels'... Could you (Brian chooses one audience member particularly vocal during the previous discussion and passes him or her a KEEP/DELETE sign) just help us set up the voting? So I'm going to read you a sample of the 800+ emails I received after announcing Purge and you're going to listen to the evidence and decide how you would vote. Don't overthink these first few (mostly keep) and just go with your gut (mostly keep) and we'll take it from there, ready?

Purge

Music: the first four seconds of Prince's 7, 1992.

PHIL

For the sake of your purge project, you may wish to remind the panel that I once took a picture of my dick and sent it to you for the sake of your art. If that's not a true facebook friend, I don't know what is...

KEEP

Good good, that was an easy one, right? Of course KEEP right? Good, now I want to tell you that there is a pattern to these first few responses... and it's not that the people are photographers.

JULIA

I just want you to know that you may tell the judges that I sensually stroked your man-bits (haha) on stage without necessarily knowing you...

KEEP

So you know, for the sake of privacy, I've anonymized all the responses I received for *Purge* with the exception of two, from whom I've asked explicit permission. I asked this next audience member if I could use her name because I think it's relevant to the proceedings. I want you to think of her name as you vote.

KARMA

Purge sounds pretty awesome. I am sure that given our connection was over clove cigarettes and your testicle in Arizona in 2004, I'll probably be purged, but it's been nice being your facebook friend.

KEEP

> **HEATHER**
> Perhaps you should mention that we proposed that you be a potential sperm donor... do you remember that night?
>
> **KEEP**

In reality, some of the 800 responses I received within three days of my posting were not about my genitals. If you can believe it.

> **ARIK**
> I'd be happy to participate in Purge. Let's stay friends — performers should stick together... However, I must say that I have hidden your status updates. You update every five minutes and it was driving me fucking crazy.
>
> **DELETE**

YES! Even though Arik was a fetish club performer in Tokyo and sometimes posted interesting — if not slightly problematic — pictures, he was one of the first Facebook friends deleted. I was sad because I was traveling to Tokyo last year and, obviously, it would be fun to have a fetish club performer take you out, but when I got there, I realized that I had changed his name for this performance, and I don't even remember his real name to contact him. It did feel good though, doesn't it feel good?

PURGE LOGO

You've wanted to do it for so long. Every time you see their face in this digital space, you cringe, you sweat, you lose a little piece of yourself. But would they notice? Do you care if they would? Why did you ever have this connection in the first place? Why are we here, together?

At this point in PURGE, an audience member comes up and deletes one friend from their social network.[9]

Good work. (*Brian hands out more KEEP/DELETE signs.*) So now let's democratize a bit more. In a way, the entire *Purge* project was meant to help me understand people's standards and organizing principles around social networking. Perhaps by doing this all together, we'll find a method for who should be connected to whom... and you'll get to see how these panels voted. Signs ready?

Music: the first four seconds of Prince's 7, 1992.

FAITH

Tell everyone that I took you out for pizza when you were visiting Tel Aviv, and tell them I paid for it too. And then tell them that I have a great rack... Let's see how they vote then!!

(*Brian will choose one or two audience members to explain their vote, before eventually announcing the result.*)

DELETE

DANIEL

What fun, Brian! I hope I'm able to watch the stream when my name comes up. I have faith in our friendship that I'll make the cut. And if not, well, it was nice

---

[9] In hopes of proving to the audience that I'm serious, at this point in the show, I always move my chair back and take a drink, staring at the audience until someone comes up. The longest I ever sat was about two minutes – eventually someone will come up. While they are signing into their account, we discuss who the person is, why they want to get rid of them, and why they ever had them in the first place. When the audience member begins typing their name, I will always put my hand over the projection – in hopes of protecting the privacy of the person discussed/deleted. When the person is deleted, there is an applause.

knowing you. I'm glad I have a bed full of pillows that
will collect my tears.

> **KEEP**

LINDSAY
Remember to establish my positive track record with
you... good times in college, recent reunion in our
adult years... before you mention that I made out with
you and didn't call the next day... or for like a year...

> **DELETE**

And then we reconnected, and then she invited me to
her wedding and I didn't go... and I didn't rsvp (I know,
I know, I'm a dick) and then I noticed that she had deleted
me. And we haven't spoken since.

YOKO
Thank you for the information about your next
performance. I don't mind you use my Facebook page
for that. Honestly I still don't get it how to use it —
personal status? Anyway in my opinion, friendship
can not be deleted by a delete button.

> **KEEP**

SANDRA
I've been thinking about this; trying to figure out why it
makes me uncomfortable to be part of this experiment
and I think it's the use of the changing jury, with no true
jury selection process. Why can't you, Brian, be the one
to decide on your own if we should be associated via this
medium? But I get it, it's 'performance art' and you are
using your Facebook friends as the raw materials. But

I don't know... we're people. I guess I find it a bit cruel to play with people's emotions surrounding rejection in the name of art. It has the potential to be mean spirited. Just by design. I guess I'm surprised by that coming from you, Brian, but maybe I don't know you very well and that's the point of this purge...

DELETE

You don't need to vote. Sandra deleted me pre-emptively. We have not spoken since, which is a shame because last year, she became a really, incredibly successful television writer. It's not that I think one should stay friends with successful people, but rather, that I really wanted to email her a message of congratulations upon reading about her success. I figured that *Purge* was behind us, and we had had some kind of connection in the past so... and then when I went to write her the message, I saw that email in the message history and I just thought 'I don't think I should speak to that person again.' And, yeah, we have not spoken since.

STEPHANIE
Purge away, my friend. I'll still be here.

KEEP

SIMONE
What are the rules after purge? If people are deleted will you consider re-adding them? Do you leave it to them to add you again as a friend? Do you decide for every single person beforehand what you are going to say? If I felt uncomfortable and pre-emptively deleted you would you be my friend again after?! I'm starting to wonder, though, whether the performance really lies in responses, Purgatory, rather than Purge, and

the waiting to be judged.

KEEP

MARTIN

Can I not delete you or un-friend you first???? Aren't I free to chose? You know what, Brian, I am going to think for a minute at some time of my own choosing as to whether to delete you or un-friend you first!!'

KEEP

Of course he should be DELETED, right? But he was kept... but I decided to delete him a few days later. I just did not need that shit in my life.

CINDY

Hi Brian, please don't 'Purge' me. You are my link to Grant outside of his family. You are the person I watch to feel connected to the Grant the rest of the world knew, the side of him I was waiting for him to let me know better. I don't communicate with anyone on Facebook but I look at your page often and love following your life in Facebook snippits.

KEEP

JENNI

I really don't think I should be de-friended. I am from Egypt and we just had a fucking revolution. Give us a fucking break.

KEEP

MOM

You don't need to vote on whether to KEEP or DELETE my mother, because my mother is not my Facebook friend...

Purge

[I have edited this section of *Purge* out of respect for my mother, but just know that what is spoken in the live performance is about digital connection and disconnection and shame and sharing between families, and the limits of sharing. While everyone else is able to be anonymized as part of this publication, it's impossible to do this with my mother, whom I adore. She is not a fictional mother, she's a real woman. And she is awesome. And she is not my Facebook friend. I think this is best for us. And I am pretty sure she agrees.]

Where was I?

1:00 Countdown (featuring a digital alarm at :00)

Ooh. It's about 2am, Chicago time, 3am, Michigan time, and Grant — who described his feelings through the lyrics of Prince songs — was worried about how late I was working. 'It's no problem, the show opens in a few days,' I said, 'But what I'm really concerned about is the shrieking studio neighbor'; 'if you don't hear from me in the morning, I've probably been axe murdered.' The banging continued to happen in the studio next door to mine, and while I hated not knowing exactly what that horrifying noise was, I mostly just thought it was someone wielding a hard-to-manage sledgehammer or something art-creation related.

The long process of goodnights was started — I vomit a little to think of my 25-year-old self doing such a thing. 'No you hang up!', 'You didn't hang up either!', 'Okay, 1,2,3...' and before it was over, my phone died. Assuredly, my cosmic karma for enacting that tragically silly, predicatable, two-young-boys-in-love stereotype.

It was 2:30am, and I headed back to do finishing touches on the set, when there was a loud knock at the door... I stopped. My heart sank and suddenly, the image of the sledgehammer-wielding maniac in the room next door came to my mind. I cautiously opened up the door. A City of Chicago Police Officer. Someone was dead.

Brian Lobel

Music: the first four seconds of Prince's 7, 1992.

TARA
Hi Brian, I have no issues with my info being shared.

DELETE

So it was weird with Tara because Tara, who I grew up with and went to high school with, was not very cool or confident growing up. She was bullied. Although she was weird just like me, I seemed to project weird outwards – acceptable for boys – while she remained weird and shy – unacceptable for girls. I felt horrible when her name came up, as I didn't have anything else to say other than 'I don't want to delete her because she wasn't very popular in high school' and didn't want to say that. So when it came about that I had nothing to say about this girl who I hadn't seen in 13 years, and who I don't know anything about... she was DELETED. Immediately I felt horrible. About two minutes later, Heidi, a friend from my high school, watching from Portland, emailed about how difficult it was to watch Tara get deleted. She understood what I wasn't saying. Later that night, however, Tara herself wrote back writing, 'You are too funny, Brian! I actually wasn't too surprised that they voted for you to un-friend me as we haven't had a ton of interaction on Facebook (or since high school).' And then she continued on... And then I noticed... the shy 17-year-old girl I was trying to protect no longer existed. She was now a 30-year-old woman, with a career, two children, a partner, and, from her most recent status update, a lease on a new blue car. Perhaps I didn't need to re-friend that 17-year-old girl, but instead needed to 'Friend' this new woman for the first time. And so I did.

GIL
Hi Brian. I was wondering if I could remain your Facebook friend but be left out of purge, please?

> The idea of me being discussed for my value (and then checking back to find I've been un-friended) doesn't really sit well with me at the moment. Maybe at other times I'd feel differently, and I know I'm taking this too seriously, but at the moment I'm needing to feel secure in my friendships and all that kind of thing. I hope you don't mind?
>
> **KEEP**

I pre-emptively Kept Gil.

> **JAMIE**
>
> I support your work and really like you. Maybe this will turn out to be a very interesting project.
>
> **Maybe.**
>
> I imagine that the responses of your various friends to the project will be considered and potentially incorporated into the piece itself. Well, my response is a feeling of being rubbed the wrong way by what struck me as an off-putting form letter, and the disturbing image of our symbolic connection being placed on the auction block over coffee. I deleted you as an exercise of my agency as a participant in your project.
>
> **DELETE**

Jamie deleted me pre-emptively. We haven't talked since.

So, Bica works the door at Dalston Superstore, and wants you to meet her so that you know that everything she says here is real. I'd like everyone here to vote because Bica's response was the only response that I received that came with an actual threat of real physical violence.

BICA

I'm defo for keeps cause: 1) You love my exotic Serbian ass. Actually I have caught you out numerous times staring at it. 2) We are sister doorwhores. Doorho's before bro's babes. 3) I'm hard as fuck and I know some shit dodgy ass people who are gonna kick the shit out of your Yankee fucking ass if you dare delete me.

KEEP

And you know that she was kept because, well, I'm here with you today.

GABRIELA (HER CHOSEN PSEUDONYM)

Okay, as for Purge, I've thought a lot about it, and decided to do the third option and tell my own story about our friendship. I'm sure that this is something I should have told you before, but there's no time like the present. You're welcome to treat this as part of your performance, but I also hope you'll take it as an honest (and uncharacteristically earnest) reflection. Here goes:

We've been friends for a long time. In fact, I don't remember ever meeting you, only having you in my life, and in fact, I think you were my first male friend. Blah, blah, blah, skip forward 20 years, college, making out, visiting Chicago, blah blah blah.

Anyway, last June, I was at a birthday party in Boston, and a friend said to me that he had just seen a video of your most recent performance, and that I was in it, and should probably check it out. You were kind enough to send it to me, and I watched it, surprised to find my full name mentioned in it, in context of having 'interacted' with your genitals after your testicular cancer surgery.

Let's say that I had some cognitive dissonance about that experience.

On the one hand, I'm an artist, right? As a writer, I feel very strongly that artistic expression is of sui generis value, plus I thought that the performance itself was good, meaningful, interesting art. There's also some sort of twisted pride that comes with being included in your public work. On the other hand, I felt surprised and somewhat uncomfortable to have my name show up in that context (even in London, even in a video in which it was *sort of* bleeped out). I wondered if I should tell you that I was uncomfortable, but I also felt, as a supporter of your work I should think of your performing self, no matter how confessional, as being something of an artificial persona, and that my name, therefore, was kind of a fiction, too. I also wondered if I would have felt differently about the whole thing if you had given me a heads up and allowed me to opt out, or choose my own pseudonym. In any case, as you know, I did nothing, and we've been in very little contact all year.

I'm not sure that my response was the right one, which I suppose is why I'm looking to have a little more voice and agency in this piece, but in defense of our Facebook and real friendship, I have these things to say. First, I feel as though we've been friends for so long that I would be very sad to have any kind of official end (no matter how symbolic) to it. Second, I feel as though we have some kind of ongoing (though dormant) conversation about ourselves as individuals and as artists, and I would like to continue it.

Actually, as I write this, I'm not at all concerned about us being Facebook friends or not, and I'll be interested to know whether or not your panelists think we ought to be. What I am concerned about is us being actual friends, and I hope that this little purge of mine will push us forward.

KEEP

And, perhaps heartbreakingly, we haven't spoken since.[10]

> **JANE**
>
> **I think what you're doing with Purge is interesting in theory. But in actual real life, I think it's kind of fucked up and hurtful to your friends, to ask strangers to tell you whether to stay friends with them and to make a game out of it. I would enjoy reading about it in a novel but that doesn't make me want to be part of it.**
>
> **DELETE**

Jane deleted me pre-emptively. We've spoken since, but it's awkard.

> **EVAN**
>
> **Thought I would drop you a line with regards to your project that I read about in the note you put on here.**
>
> **It is absolutely my wish that you do not use my profile, my name, a pseudonym for my name, this email, or any part of this email as part of the project. I assume that to facilitate at least some of this that I will need to delete you on here. Confirm if that is the case.**
>
> **Essentially I feel quite strongly about privacy, particularly my own and I've spent a considerable amount of time ensuring my very compartmentalised life stayed as such. You are the only person I have**

---

[10] This statement was true when *Purge* was performed in 2013, but Gabriela and I have since spoken and are in touch quite regularly. The line, however, remains the same in performance today – despite it not being factually true. I was quite gutted that this email – and us getting back in touch – had not immediately resulted in a perfectly rekindled friendship. And I wanted to make it clear to audiences that even though *Purge* rekindled many friendships, these friendships demand constant attention and commitment from both people.

encountered who has used reference to me in such a public context that has made me feel unhappy. I appreciate that knowing you has been a two way relationship and I cannot have any control over how you choose to recall that relationship. On the other hand, if you have any consideration for the integrity of that relationship, I would ask that you respect my wishes.

DELETE

MARTIN
I think you put too much faith in democracy to yield the correct result.

KEEP

First Friendster message from Grant, April 14, 2005

Subject: If you're down with P, then you're down with me[11]

Brian,

Thanks again for the tix on Friday. When people ask about my trip to Chicago I say 'I saw a play on land reform – no really, it was great!!' The fact that John Malkovich was in it seems to impress them – as well it might – but really, the play's theme of liberal optimism's unintended consequences is what I really groove on. Eff. There I go again. Immediately after I said the words 'The Treaty of Westphalia' at dinner with you and Priya I felt as if I had just pulled a trigger. 'He died of a self-inflicted gunshot wound' the paper would read. I asked Priya if I came off as the Scoutmaster of the Nerd Patrol. She demurred.

But it was great hanging out and I really enjoy poaching Priya's friends. Keep an eye on her, report embarrassing

---

[11] We had hoped to find the original font for Friendster to be used here, but this appears currently unavailable. You can, however, use your imagination about an early 2000s social networking font.

stories back to me, and try not to let her have moral crises where none exist.

Yours,

Grant

It's Complicated

When I was doing *Purge,* I was overwhelmed with emails and phone calls and angry messages and so so many people getting in touch. As I was walking home from the installation, many days I couldn't even stop thinking and talking about people from my past, from here, from there, from cancer world, and from childhood, from one-night stands, from family... And in the middle of this all, on the third night of my installation, I woke up in a cold sweat, nervous that I had gotten my history with Grant wrong.

So, Friendster had introduced the term 'It's Complicated' as an option for one's Relationship Status, and Grant had selected it, in 2006, after our first break up. I remember thinking, IT'S NOT COMPLICATED, IT'S OVER. And I remember being 25, and I remember being an idiot. But what I don't remember, and what woke me in this cold sweat was, if maybe, in the middle of the night, one night in 2006, I just opened up my computer and deleted him, just so I wouldn't have to see that complication, or be reminded of that complication, which would exist from 2006 until his death, and which still exists today.

Music: the first four seconds of Prince's 7, 1992.

> **WINSTON**
> **When I was a puppy, Grant giggled at my curly tail (it is almost a double-curl not that I'm bragging) and my flat face. Hope you and the panel will keep me as a furry friend of Facebook forever. Yours truly, Winston the Dog**
>
> **KEEP**

GERALD

Will I be purged? Its almost like I want to be purged. Is there a number you want to get your friends down to? 1342 friends is an awful lot. Apparently the average is 150, something to do with primate grouping structures. Gerry. PS – Please do not purge me, Please do not purge me, Please do not purge me, Please do not purge me, Please do not purge me.

DELETE

We have since re-friended, but he has not forgotten.

STATUS UPDATES IMMEDIATELY FOLLOWING THE PURGE:

Brian Lobel: the PURGE is over.

Brian Lobel shall never repeat the PURGE again.

Brian Lobel has been dependent on the good humor of many friends.

Brian Lobel cannot thank his friends enough for helping him get through it. And for helping him get through everything else.

PURGE LOGO

I don't know if Grant deleted me, or I deleted him. I'm not sure if it is, necessarily, important. I'd like to think it isn't. I'd like to think it isn't because — when both users are still alive, at least — it is just as easy to reconnect these severed ties. Just as easy to reconnect and repair. To mend, with the click of a button. It is hard to do — sometimes it's hard because we're hurt, sometimes it's hard because we were responsible for hurting. But the action – typing the name and then clicking ADD AS A FRIEND – is actually just as simple, if we let it be...

At this point in PURGE, audience members shout out the kinds of people they would contact, add or re-add to their social network, if they could.

*(Music: Prince's *7*, 1992, full length.) And if someone wants to contact, add or re-add one of their contacts, they do. And we watch, supportively*[12]

DWELLING

I've spent tonight trying so hard to think about Grant for one minute. We're all told it's good to reflect, to keep gratitude journals, to think about what's really important, but I find that, if I really want to remember something, I need to think about it out loud, or to type it out and read and reread it – I've even written this story about Grant down so that I don't get distracted.

It's hard to think of someone for one minute, or it is for me. I find it hard to dwell. Perhaps this is because of the rapid nature of this world that includes things like social networking. Perhaps it's chemical, as I'm sure I have some attention deficits one way or another, or perhaps I just keep choosing the wrong person to reflect on. I find that my mind, around 40 seconds in, starts to wander. But it's just a minute, and I'd like you to try it with me. I've been talking and talking and talking about Grant, who is not relevant to you – I mean, maybe you feel like you know him a bit after I've talked about him so much… but I know that you have people in your own life who are more meaningful to you. So I'll just ask you to select someone to think about, someone for whom thinking about them for one minute would be woefully inadequate. Someone you could think about forever and ever. Close your eyes, don't look at the clock, and just try to dwell. Once you've selected your person, close your eyes, and I'll start the clock. I'm going to try my best, too.

---

[12] Unlike the first time when there was a similar ask, I do not stay silent for too long with this request. About 50% of the time someone will come on stage and re-add or contact an old friend and 50% of the time there will be silence – which I'm fine with also. If no one comes up, after the chorus of *7*, I put up an optional next slide reading: **And if not, that's ok too.**

Purge

1:00 Countdown (featuring a digital alarm at :00)

In May 2011, Friendster deleted all of its user content, but until then, and particularly because no one checked or monitored it, Grant had stayed virtually alive.

Image of Grant's Friendster Profile

On his Friendster page, he was 30, male, living in Chicago and single. Even if our Friendster-ship had been severed, I was so happy to see him there.

1:00 Countdown

The long process of goodnights was started — I vomit a little in my mouth to think of my 25-year-old self doing such a thing. 'No you hang up!', 'You didn't hang up either!', 'Okay, 1,2,3..' and before it was over, my phone died. Assuredly, my cosmic karma for enacting that tragically silly, predicatable, two-young-boys-in-love stereotype.

It was 3:30am, and I headed back to do finishing touches on the set. I'm sure that I could have been out of the studio by 1, had I not spent the entire time talking with Grant, but it made me feel buoyant and confident, so I didn't mind the lateness. There was a loud knock at the door... I stopped. My heart sank and suddenly, the image of the sledgehammer-wielding maniac in the room next door came to my mind. I cautiously opened up the door. A City of Chicago Police Officer. Someone was dead.

'Are you Brian Lobel', he asked sternly?

'Yes, I am.'

'Marc at the front told me you'd be back here. Well, someone in East Lansing, Michigan, is worried about you. He said that you thought you were going to get murdered and then your phone cut out.'

'My phone died, I was talking too much.'

'Yeah, he said he thought that might be the case... but he was worried.'

'Well I don't have my charger, and his number...'
'I have his number here. You can call your boyfriend with my phone.'
'Thanks.'

(Brian smiles. The alarm plays – it is the opening of Prince's 'Starfish and Coffee', 1987. Lights down. The End.)

Purge at SummerWorks Festival, Toronto
Photo by Tania El Khoury, 2012

Purge at NUS Arts Festival 2016, Singapore
Photo by Uyên Diệp, courtesy of NUS Centre For the Arts

Sample Opening Status Updates

Each performance of *Purge* began with five to ten minutes of writing a real Facebook status while the audience got settled. As people are so familiar with the FB interface, it often took people a few minutes to figure out what was actually happening, what I was actually doing. I was watching, responding, and spending these first critical minutes of a show (hopefully) building a rapport with the audience. While each status update is different there are a few key characteristics: a desire to be live in the space and to respond to who's actually there and how it feels, discussion of my shoes (which would often solicit a cheer from the audience), a handing out of beer (to encourage audience participation) and an invitation to viewers at home to watch *Purge* on the livestream.

The livestream of *Purge* was never made public outside of my Facebook community, not during the installation itself or any of the public performances. The livestream was not about racking up thousands or millions of viewers, but instead about practicing radical accountability to the people who were being discussed. Because my Facebook friends had participated in *Purge*, it was my commitment that they always be able to watch the show for free. As I quickly open the webpage with the livestream in front of the live audience, I hope that the presence of this virtual community demonstrates my commitment and love to people in both virtual and corporeal space.

The following are a few sample updates. The length of the update usually depends on how long it takes to get an audience settled, how long Front of House wants me to hold before the show starts, and, of course, how I'm feeling (e.g. how rant-filled or rage-filled or love-filled I feel on a particular day).

Infecting the City, Cape Town | March 13, 2014
is just about to start PURGE, Cape Town. AHHHHH so fun. The audience is about 1:45hr late, but I'm SOOOO glad they're

here. You're awesome for being here. I heard the dance was awesome. Was it awesome? Do you think this show will be as good? I am not a competitive person... but they will be different. For sure.

Come on in, come on in. Is the song 'That's what friends are for' big here? Is it culturally relevant? Do you know and care about Dionne Warwick like I do? I hope you do. Does anyone want a beer? I have one. Come up and get it. The other is mine. You should feel free to scooch up if you want to. In your chairs.

Lovely group of people – this group in the front row is definitely reading, and I appreciate that. Readers. I'm not a big reader myself, but I am glad you are. NOT YOU! The other front row. I just want to start a little pre-game competition. Soz. Is that a word here? Soz it's like London for 'sorry' because londoners can't be bothered to pronounce both syllables. They are quite lazy, but I like them. Can the first rows (both of you) (the winners and the losers of the original competition) move your rows up like a metre? And then can everyone follow them? And while you do that... can you sing along? THATS.... ENOUGH. This is my show, not yours. Just kidding. It's OUR show. This will be fun. I'm glad you're here. If you can't see you can come and sit on the floor. In the front. And if you're struggling, then you should move in the front.

If you prefer a side view (warning: lots of Brian's profile, which is nose-y) there are seats. I love a big nose. Can you handle it? Come on... live a little. Don't just stand there. Move it.

Don't stand in the back, there are seats right there. And I want you CLOSE!!!!! CCCCCLLLLOOOOSSSSEEEE! You. You. You. I'm staring at you. Move. : (Just kidding.

Are you ready to start? Can I get a whoop whoop? Awesome. This is kind of a sad show, but I'll try to make it funny. Promise. But it's 45 minutes, and I'm just next to the bathroom... so if you have to go, just go. And if you want a beer, just get a beer. At any time. I'm just about ready.

Are you READY!?!??! YEAH!!!One more time. All together in 5, 4, 3, 2, 1, .OK. Let's do it! xxxx

and friends at home, as always you can watch on the live stream:

http://ustream.tv/channel/brianlobelpurge

Brighton Dome Studio for Brighton Festival | May 19, 2014
is just about to start PURGE in Brighton, for Brighton Festival 2014. WOOHOO! We'll always be together. LOVE NEVER ENDS. Don't be afraid to sing along. So, I've just finished five days of working at the Dome, doing my Mourning Glory Trilogy, which went well, I think. I hope people liked it...

The thing I heard the most was that people at the Brighton Festival remembered me from my previous performances at Brighton Festival, the last one which involved over 500 people touching my genitals. This is not that performance. If you want your ticket back now is the time. Sorry. Just kidding this one is better. I think. You would hope to think that. Hi David. So there's no genitals, well, none seen, but some discussed. I hope that's ok. Is that okay? I can't hear you. Is that ok? Good.

Does anyone want a beer? Raise your hand. Audience participation pays... This is what we call positive reinforcement.

Do you know this song? It was bigger in the US, I think. But if you know it... will you please sing along? That'd be great.

So the only thing that is a real tragedy about today is that this desk that I'm sat at is covered in fabric... so I can't show you the AWESOME shoes I am wearing. Do you want to see them? Do you???All together. 3.2.1. YEAH> you fucking betcha. Hi hi hi you're not late. You're on time. We've just been having some fun. Anyone else want a beer say HAY! 3.2.

PARTICIPATION ROCKS.

I'm so glad you're all here.

Just a quick shoutout to my flatmate... if you could wait a few minutes after the show... i have a box for you to take home.

Sample Opening Status Updates

Awesome.

Now back to the show. Can you sing along? SWAYI'll BE ON YOUR SIDE FOREVER MORE>>>>>>>>

ORLA!!!!!!!!!!!!!!!!!

Keep Smiling. Keep shining.

For sure.

Ok. So it's looks like we're almost ready to go, I'm so excited. I love Brighton. I love Brighton Festival. But note, this is not like my other Brighton Festival show... no genitals, sorry.

After the show... that's another story....

stragglers. Just kidding, they're on time. But I love you all more. SHHHHHHH Don't tell them.

Hi. That's what friends are for.... yeah. That impulse to sing.... louder. THAT's WHAT FRINEDS ARE FOR!!!!

My typing is terrible sorry. Blerg. It's been a big week. So glad you're here. I said. That. But I mean it. IT's MY SHOW NOT YOURS!!!!!!!

Just kidding. Its' your show too.

Ok, and if you're watching at home, as always, I'll see you in a bit.

www.ustream.tv/channel/brianlobelpurge

xxo.

New Wolsey Theatre for PULSE14 | June 7, 2014

is just about to start PURGE: Ipswich, the final show in the UK of Purge for a while. Phew, it's been a while... but I'm really excited to be back in Ipswich. Hi. Welcome. Sit close. We're all friends here, for now.

If you sit in the front row, you can have one of the beers on the table. That's good encouragement isn't it? Do you know this song? That's what firends are for.... Dione Warwick. Classic. Well you came and opened me. Hi welcome.

Ipswich seems nice. Are you nice? YES? No?!? Quiet group. Hello! Can you see me? Does anyone want a soft drink? It's coconut juice... No one? I guess the coconut juice fad is over. Beer?

First person with a hand up.

See audience participation pays. Literally. Figuratively all of it. So last time I performed in Ipswich was 2011, so it's nice to be back. Welcome. Hi.

That's what friends are for..........

So, still a few people to come in... Hi. You're not late. I'm early. Usually, the lighting shows off my shoes... but not tonight... which sucks, because I had them resoled for the occasion. Wanna see? Wanna see? Let me hear you say YEAH! Come on, you can do better. 1, 2, 3, YEAH! Green. Thanks.

Wow, lots of people, but still no one in the front row, who will automatically get a free beer. Positive reinforcement. And now another, but no more beer. Soz.

Soz.

Does anyone know this song? LET ME HEAR YOU !!!!!!!! Blond. FOR SURE.

So this is my show and I think we're about ready to go.

If you saw me earlier at Nic's show, I wasn't trying to be rude, by leaving after it was over – which is a funny thing to say – but I had to get back to prep. So I wasn't being rude. Promise. I fucking loved that show. It was so quiet and nice. This is not quiet. I hope it's nice. SING .... .KEEEP SMILING. KEEP SHINING . KNOWING YOU CAN ALWAYS COUNT ON ME. FOR SURE.

for the good times. I am a good touch typer. I would like to thank Mrs. Joan Linford who taught me touch typing when I was 12.

So here we go...

And if you're watching at home, as always, you can watch here: www.ustream.tv/channel/brianlobelpurge

See you in an hour.

Live Art Bistro (LAB), Leeds | January 22, 2015

is just about to start PURGE: LEEDS @ LAB. YEAH LAB, I like

it here. I mean, I do wish more people would sit closer, but that's ok. MOVE UP. SEE ALL THESE EMPTY SEATS??? COME ON>>>>

I promise not to bully anyone during the show... unless no one moves up. In which case, all promises are off. You'll want to be able to see the screen. Can you see the screen? Great. Do you know the words? SING!

That's what friends are for.... duooo du du du du duduuuuu well yo.

Anyway, it's so

SHUT UP ADAM. I'm TRYING TO START. DON'T TAG ME IN THINGS NOW.

So, this will be so nice...

I love LEeds. Does leeds love me???? YEAH!!

That's good..

So who wants a free beer? Handsu p.

See how easy participation is???

Who wants a cider?

in good times, and bad tiems??

this is the worst typing ever.

SING... KEE SMILING KEEP SHING FOR SURE.

Ok they seem warmed up, a bit. Let's see how we go...

And you at home, you can always watch...

www.ustream.tv/channel/brianlobelpurge

See you in a bit. xxx

Off Center, Fusebox, Austin | April 11, 2015

loves Austin so so much. Just about to start the 2nd and final show of PURGE: Austin, after 4 days of live purging from the amazing Jeff Mills and the splendiferous Kymberlie Quong Charles. They were amazing. And now it's time for the stage show... I hope you all like it...

The doors are open and people are starting to come in. Hi, welcome welcome. So glad you're here. Come in. Sit down, get comfy. Welcome. We'll always be together. It's a nice looking audience thus far. Some nice beards, some nice print... YEAH REBECCA!!!!!!!!!!!!!!!!!!!!!!! I'm so glad you got here. That's great news. Hello hello. Welcome. Sit down. I'm glad you're here. Sit down.

Does everyone have a drink that wants one? Do you want a beer? Does anyone want a beer? Grab it. See how easy audience participation is? That was fun. Oh come in, come NOW SIT DOWN. This is my show. Not yours. Just kidding. Love you. Welcome.

Did you get a beer if you want one? One left..... no one... More for me, that's ok.

So, I hope you'll sing along to this song. When I travel and perform this elsewhere in the world they don't know it. But you should. Do you? I hope you do. ...

And I, never thoguht I 'd feel this way.

I have to say I'm very sad that my friend Divya could not be here tonight, because her babysitter cancelled just a few minutes ago. Let's take a moment for Divya, shall we. ? Now sing.

FOR SURE.

Thta'ts thwat friends are for.... For good times, and bad times. I'll be onyours side forever more... I took touchtyping class in middle school. Big up to Mrs. Linford, Bethlehem Central Middle School. She was epic.

And so by the way I thank you. Comfy? Feeling good? Have you seen my shoes? I'll show you. FANCY . fjust for you.

Keepsmiling keeLOUDER. FOR SURE1

That's what friends are for.... we are going to starti n a moment, so sing sing sing... THAT WHAT FRIENDS ARE OOHHHHHOOOOOO.

Keep shining. FOR SURE.

There's one more beer in case anyone wants.... no? Pass this to him.

SEE ?! Audience participation is awesome.

Sample Opening Status Updates

FOR the good times, and the bad times. I'll be on your side forever more.

Seriously, these lyrics are actually profound, I think. If you don't think so... we might have a bad time together. Just kidding. I'll love you anyway.

And you... at home, are of course welcome to watch where you are: www.ustream.tv/channel/brianlobel

Austin: PUrge, here we go. x

Old Folks Association, Auckland | March 17, 2016

I hope that you in the audience are not offended that I still have the 'Australia' image up in my FB. Usually I try to have a 'local' image, but my computer died between Sydney and Auckland. It just got fixed today, but I didn't get to think of something really quirky and adorable about New Zealand. I was thinking of something about Whale Rider, but that feels uninformed, or out of date. Sorry. But as you notice, Muriel's Wedding is pretty out of date too... but I still think it's the best image from Australian cinema...

Ok, so we are really about to start, and I'm so excited you're here.

This is my first performance in New Zealand. YEAH! YEAH!!!! WOOHOO!! LET ME HEAR YOU!!!! GREAT.

Thanks. Today, I posted a post about how this was the first time in a long time that I've performed in a country that does not have institutionalised homophobia... therefore... THIS SHOW WILL BE SUPER GAY!!!! SUPER GAY!!!! I HOPE YOU LIKE THAT! DO YOU LIKE IT??? that sounded ok. but not great... DO YOU LIKE IT!!?!?!?! BETTER. Thank you.

Does anyone need a beer? Does anyone need another beer for later? No? Nothing?

See audience participation is easy. And you get beer! Or an awesome performance experience... so good.

Do you know this song? Or am I too old? SING!!!!!!!! OOOHHHHH

HH HH H H KEEP MSILING KEEP SINIGN NOWING YOU CAN
ALWAYS COOUNT MON MY horrible typer horrible typer.

So we're going to start at the end of this song... and for those
who were early... sorry you had to hear it many times.s...
thissi is my favorite part.

Anyone else need a beer? Hands up? No. No.... Phew. If you
get thirsty in the show... just grab it anytime.

Ok time to start. Start proper.

And for you all at home... the NEW ZEALAND PREMIERE OF
PURGE STARTS NOW!!!

NUS Arts Festival, Singapore | March 24, 2016

is about to start the SINGAPORE PREMIERE of PURGE! Aren't
you excited? I am. Good cheer. I like that. So before we get
to that business... you can talk through this part, don't worry.
We won't start for a bit still. It's not time yet.

First, what's on my mind today. Obviously, everyone is thinking
about Brussels, which is just so messed up and terrible.
That's happening, I'm thinking of that. AND OF COURSE i'm
thinking about all the amazing work all the disability activists
are doing in London... ooh, so radical, so important. The
UK government is totally f*cking disabled people and their
benefits, that sucks. SO YEAH TO THE PROTESTERS. YEAH!

Anyway, let's be more local... another thing I'm thinking about
is my hair... which still hasn't really adjusted to the humidity.
Are there any other curly girls who have this problem?
RESPECT. Mad respect.

I love Singapore, so far. FRIED CHICKEN FOR BREAKFAST!!!!

That's one good thing. And I like that here Eco before a word
can mean EITHER ecological OR economical. That's a weird
post-capitalist something that I'm still figuring out. But I'm
into it.

Oh I also find the people SUPER friendly. Arne't you? YEAH!
Ok ok. I want to be friendly too. Does anyone want a beer?

I also want one.

anyone else want?

SEE HOW EASY AUDIENCE PARTICIPATION IS???? ? AND YOU GET THINGS. Awesome.

Do you know this song? SING IF YOU DO. I'll wait until there's a good moment, then I'll cue you in...

Oh, warnings... this show c FOR SUIRE. THAT's WAHT AFRIENDS ARE FOR>>>>>> IN GOOD TIMES. AND BaD TIMES   I'LLLASDLFKAJSDLFKJASLKAJSDFLKAJSDFLKJAS That's what friends are for.....

Warnings... now for the serious part, but you can keep singing, so it sounds less serious....

THIS SHOW CONTAINS ADULT LANGUAGE. FUCK. SHIT. PISSS. Is that ok? If not, you can leave. I'll pay for your ticket. Serious. I don't want you offended. well, I do want you offended, but I don't want you in my audience. Awesome.

ALSO. THIS SHOW HAS SOME SEXUAL CONTENT. As they say here... some 'connotations of homosexuality'. THERE WILL BE NO CONNOTATIONS. I WILL TALK VERY FREELY. Is that ok? YEAH?! Great...

I'm not done yet... so you get to hear this another second. NO CONNOTATIONS. REAL TALK ABOUT PRETTY GAY THINGS. I HOPE THAT'S OK/ If you're offended... go NOW! I will pay for your ticket. Thank you for making me feel so welcomed, otherwise. No one? I brought cash, just in case... ok. Your silence means its ok!!! That's a horrible policy that I would never encourage about anything, except for this. Thanks.

That's what friends are for....

Ok, I think we're just about ready... Everyone has a seat. A few adorable people on the side of the main seating section. HOWDY!!! I LOVE YOU!!!! Don't worry if you're sitting in the middle. I LOVE YOU TOOOOOO!!!!

Ok, it's time to go. The show is 50ish minutes from here...

Maybe 60. Depends on you. You'll be talking and listening, I hope you can do both. I hear great things about how smart people are here.

So let's do it. KEEP MSILING KEEP SHINGING. SING!!!!!!!!!!!! Fo sure. That's what friends are for...

And if you're watching at home, as usual, you can watch here: www.ustream.tv/channels/brianlobelpurge

Lez do this!

Malthouse Theatre, Melbourne | March 30, 2016

is just about to start the Australian premier (premiere? sp?!?) of PURGE – here in Melbourne, at the Malthouse. You can see the homage to Australianness in my profile picture. I thought that Muriel's Wedding homage would be a cheap shot... but ABBA WAS ALWAYS PLAYING AT THE HOTEL I AM STAYING AT. Meaning that it's totally appropriate.

Get comfy. Here we go. Ooh, I'm nervous that my spelling is shit today – soz. This intro might be painful if my spelling is shit but asd;flkajsdg;laksjd;alksdjh l;kahj forget it. It matters what's communicated, not the spelling, right? That's what I told my teachers.

Get comfy, get comfy. Before I start I should say a bit of what's on my mind today. It's Wednesday, 2016, March, and I'm thinking about Trump, and Bernie, and Hillary and Broad City, I love broad city, and I'm so annoyed that Australian time is so far behind (or ahead?) of America... that I have to wait until Friday to download an episode. THESE ARE SERIOUS PROBLEMS!!!! I'm sure you understand.

I'm also thinking about Turkey, and Brussels and Pakistan, and a bunch of my friends who are, today, having surgery. I hope they have a good/ok time and that htey are safe.

Ooh ,my favorite song. I hope you like it too. Feel free to sing along.

SIT CLOSER!!!!!!!!!!!!! THAT'S SO FAR AWAY!!!!!!! WHY

Sample Opening Status Updates

DON'T YOU LOVE ME?!?!?!?!?

You can't see my shoes so far away, can you??? They are nice shoes right? I can't hear you. Are they nice shoes? YEAH!!! THANK YOU!!!! Do you want a beer?

See audience participation is EASY?!!!!! AND YOU GET THINGS. Anyone for a soft drink???? No i didn't think sol Another beer later... look out for it.

Ok... second day in Melbourne and I like it here. Lovely people. Good coffee... if not all a bit intense about HOW AWESOME THE COFFEE IS HERE. Am I right? I mean, seriously... .

But I also like that Melbourne – and Australia – is gay-friendly. EYAH!!! That's good because the last few places I've performed have been homophobic (BOOOOOOOOOOOOOOO!!!) I KNOW!!! So, this version will be SUPER GAY. I hope you don't mind.

But how gay??? I don't know... do you know the words???? SING!!!!!!!! KEEP SMILING KEEP SHINING KNOWING YOU CAN ALWAYS COUNT ON ME.... FOR SURE. THAT's WHAT FRIENDS ARE FOR>.... GOOD.

CAn everyone see my shoes? That's all the spectacle in this perforamcne.... so look close.

Eeks I'm so excited. But I 'm not done...You get more of a chance to sing if you want....

And who. wants. a. beer? Natasha sets an example for all of us. Participate and you will be rewarded. Handsomely. Handsomely.

Ok, enough fucking talking. Or typing. Oh I'm drunk. Just kidding. I'm sober. I hope you are too. No one should Purge their friends when drunk. This was a rule I don't talk about in the show, but it's important. Note it. We can talk about it later.

OK LET'S DO THIS!!!

And for those of you watching at home, as always you can watch:www.ustream.tv/channels/brianlobelpurge

Lez do this!

Additional Emails from *Purge*

Out of 800+ responses to *Purge*, only a limited number were able to be included into the script, which edits them into an order in hopes of having a dramaturgical impact. But so many of the emails that were received were so brilliant that I wanted to include them here. While nearly all of the people identified are identified by their real name – as per their permission – those whose authors could not be contacted have been anonymized. Some responses have been edited slightly for clarity or to protect sensitive information, but the original tone, spelling and punctuation have been kept.

Timothy:
i was already looking forward to this event after you told me about it back in march, when i last saw you. i trust you will use your persuasive abilities to the utmost. no doubt i will be KEPT. this will be an amazing event and i'm honored to be integral as an example of the fact that some cases are just very clear-cut. (Timothy was purged, we have since re-friended.)

Simone (full email):
Wow, this project must have caused quite a stir! I have a few questions: What are the rules after purge? If people are deleted will you consider re-adding them? Do you leave it to them to add you again as a friend? Do you decide for every single person beforehand what you are going to say? Or are you improvising on the day? If I felt uncomfortable and pre-emptively deleted you would you be my friend again after?!

The reason I'm asking this is because it does make me feel a little uncomfortable, mostly, selfishly(?), probably, because it has amplified my fragile ego and I think that although I realise my fate would be decided by strangers, you are the one that has to defend our facebook friendship, and I think that if I was deleted, I'd actually be a little upset! Although I admire the stoicism/faith/arrogance/indifference etc. etc. of those willing to be judged by a panel and potentially having this particular, cyber-connection obliterated, I'm still hesitant... and feel like a bit of a wimp!

I'm starting to wonder whether the moment of Purge will actually ever happen at all, and the performance lies in responses, Purgatory, rather than Purge, and the waiting to be judged. (Simone was kept.)

Shannon:
Should my profile come before the panel, and should you be asked to speak to the panel to contribute information which may or may not influence whether they choose to let the Facebook ax fall on my virtual neck, I would like the record to show that I enjoy being your Facebook friend not because the FB friendship as a system is anything particularly real or meaningful, but because it's one more connection to a person that I think is fun and fascinating (and I hope the other way around too, but I'm in no position of authority to speak to that). Though the connection may be small, it could be the butterfly that beats its wings in California to one day cause a monsoon is Asia. (Or would it be a typhoon? Or a hurricane? I will look it up. ....it is a typhoon.) How else would I have found out about this particular project of yours, for example? And what other life-enriching goodies are on the horizon? Perhaps I can offer you something of value one day, too. Who knows what? Maybe a picture of a turtle in a funny hat. (A picture of a turtle in a funny hat was attached to the email. Shannon was kept.)

Zach:

Got your facebook note – it sounds like a great project! However, I'd like to not take part in it, if that's okay by you... the internet is a strange enough place and privacy is hard enough to come by as it is. If it's okay with you, I think I'll de-friend you for the time being and then re-friend you on July 11. I'm sure you can understand why! It's obviously not about not trusting you (seriously, I think this actually sounds like a really cool project and I would trust you completely with my info) but I'd rather not have strangers looking at my info. (Zach purged me pre-emptively, and promptly re-added me on July 11.)

Sara:

what does it say about our relationship that I want to sit the next table over and covertly observe your production of our friendship and the ensuing response? oddly, that fishbowl experience doesn't appeal in a remote digital stream the way it would face to face. you know, unlike our almost entirely digital corrospondence these days. twisted. (Sara was kept.)

Promise:

On consecutive weekends in Jerusalem, we went to a drag show and Shabbat dinner together. (Promise was kept.)

Melanie:

Anyway, purge sounds interesting. It'd be okay if we weren't facebook friends; we're friends. And, you've never not emailed me back :) (Melanie was kept.)

Lyall:
bored already !! get on with it ...... (Lyall was purged, which was awkward because he was my boss at the time. We have since re-friended.)

Lena:
So what is a facebook friend? If it is someone you have known in real life and are connected to, then yes, we are facebook friends. If it is someone you socialize with online, then no, we are not very active facebook friends. That said, I have no way of knowing to what extent you have spent your evenings poring over my facebook page; maybe that made you feel really connected to me, and like we were visiting all the time. Was I looking at yours? You don't know. (Lena was kept.)

Kenne:
purge has awakened more narcissism inside me than i ever cared to acknowledge. Must. Hear. Friend. Defense. (Kenne was kept.)

Stella:
I'm really not sure what my un/dis-ease with it is, I guess because I sometimes discuss quite personal stuff on fb, and so that feels odd to be re-produced elsewhere. or fuck it, maybe I just don't want a bunch of strangers to decide (in public) that I'm a wanker. maybe I'd prefer it if they did (do) that in the privacy of their own homes & computers! (Stella was kept pre-emptively and did not appear in front of the panel.)

Jesse:

I petition my non-deletion because we would never see one another if not for facebook event invitations, and in a distant, admiration-of-your-work-and-chops kind of way I value your part in my life and what our virtual networks say about our respective social currencies. Um. And now I look at it, that doesn't seem like a good enough reason to stay facebooked. But Facebook itself is beside the point; although through this Purge you might end up with a lot of messages like this:

"Hi Brian, we never see one another and weren't ever really friends anyway, but I kinda like knowing you're around and that's what Facebook's good for."

That's all I've got to say, really. (Jesse was kept.)

Frank:

Re: PURGE – I think this is a fascinating, curious and exciting idea, and I love it – and I am not at all surprised that you would be involved in such a thing!

NOT as an attack, but as responsive questions, the likes of which are, I trust, part of the intention of the performance: What does it say about our society, our community, the role of social networking in our lives, that someone may allow three random people 60 seconds to determine their friendship? Is the social network itself, or the random extension thereof, a greater determinant of who our friends are (or "should" be) than our own selves? When and how and why do we cede control over our lives to a mob, or even three strangers? What role(s) might the "tipping point" and "rule of 150" concepts play in this process? When, on occasion, I find myself questioning the value of my work (and sometimes life, in a broader sense), one of the memories I turn to is walking up the stairs from the auditorium to the side hallway at BC, following closing (I'm pretty sure) night of "Cinderella" ... a young man (a 7th grader) ran up to me and said, "Mr. L, I'm *so* happy I decided to work backstage for this show! Next year, I'm going to audition!" That young man auditioned the next year, and I remember very clearly looking at my colleagues, and saying, "Where has *this* kid been hiding?!" A young man who had never acted in theater before was cast as the Jester, as clearly as if he were standing on stage in front of me at this very moment, and I can see him singing and dancing his way through "Very Soft Shoes". Makes me cry to remember it ... and makes me believe that my work (and life, in a broader sense) has been of value after all. (Frank was kept, as were all of my former teachers.)

Dan:
trying not to take it personally... but I'm fragile (Dan was purged, and we did not speak for a while. We have since re-friended.)

Brian:
Stupid and irritating. (Brian was purged.)

Robyn:
I didn't know you did this. Do you tell people how my skirt fell down in 8th grade and you were the only one to see it???? Am I really surprised we both turned out gay??? (Robyn was kept.)

Cathy:
If I'm purged, you'll be receiving a friend request from me immediately thereafter. (Cathy was kept.)

Alyssa:

I wasn't going to formally respond to your project Purge because you know I fully support your efforts. However I now write to you having been de-friended by yet another mutual friend of an ex-boyfriend. And it got me thinking about our relationship. Admittedly, I am hurt. I really liked this person and even though we weren't close friends, we both had a mutual admiration for each other. She didn't de-friend me right away, like when my ex and I actually broke it off, but later on, when we had some after-relationship drama. I can guess what drama her de-friending was based on, and a little voice in my head say, "Wait! That's not fair! You don't know my side of it!". I'm pissed! I get the choosing sides after a break up, but c'mon...why now?

So...I guess what I want to say is with your project, at least I get a fair trial. You've given me the opportunity to speak my piece, will present that and other evidence to an impartial jury. If I'm de-friended, it won't be a casual decision made in the dead of night, planted to surprise me in a few months time when I bother to check on our status. And even if I'm de-friended, I'll still know that we're friends in real life, and that I'll always get to tell you my side of the story. (Alyssa was kept. Her ex and her got back together and were married in 2014. She is still no longer Facebook friends with the woman who de-friended her.)

David:

Where to begin? I love the concept behind Purge. I've been talking to people about it since I got the message. And I'm excited to be a participant, although I've got a sneaking suspicion that I'm an easy cut.

It's been many years since we saw each other, and more since we had what I think most would consider an active, meaningful friendship. I do have lots of substantive memories of our friendship as kids though. I remember playing Nintendo in your basement, and pool, and live action Double Dare, using physical challenges constructed by your brother (that last one left an indelible impression). Racing around the neighborhood exploring construction sites and backyards. I believe I first watched the movie Labyrinth at your house, and was thus introduced to David Bowie -- that has to count for something, right? In high school, even though we were already drifting apart, I do remember continuing to admire your many theatrical and musical talents from afar, and I have distinct memories of your senior recital (you played Blue Rondo a la Turk, I believe).

With all that said, I do think our friendship is a great example of one that takes on a funny character in the age of social media. Although I do hear about you periodically via various mutual friends, we would probably not be "in touch" at all were it not for Facebook, which for you and me is actually not really being in touch at all anyway. However, I do appreciate the capabilities of the internet and social networking when it comes to an old friend like you, because you are always doing unique and thought-provoking projects, and I love reading about them. For someone not in the fine arts world, it is edifying to have friends who are, that I can sort of live vicariously through or at least count on for a little exposure to cool and novel things that are happening out there. On top of all that, you live in London, so your updates and your life are generally more mind-expanding and interesting to me than someone in New York or a more familiar life situation.

I suppose that if I were a real Facebook devotee, I might look at our "friendship" as one that has no real current content to it, and deem it a quick purge. But I am an ambivalent and infrequent user of Facebook and social media, and as such I don't think I attach much significance to the status "Facebook friend" -- if we get something out of being friends online, that's good enough for me. And I am pretty sure that I do, even though you might deem what I'm getting out of it as being pretty voyeuristic. (Maybe you have a similar voyeuristic relationship with me, but I doubt it -- I have a much less interesting online presence!)

To make sure the information exchange is in fact going both ways, here's a little about where I'm at in life right now: [The following was about 150 words of personal material which are removed in publication for privacy reasons.]

I will say that one nice thing about social networking is its ability to keep people connected enough that when the opportunity arises to kick the friendship back up to a more substantial and real level, it is more accessible and easier to do so. E.g., if I were to move to London next year, I'd know you were there (or not), and what you were up to, and I think that might make me more likely to seek you out for a cup of coffee. And then the level of familiarity that Facebook has allowed us to maintain with each other, no matter how superficial, might increase the likelihood that our friendship would be rekindled.

I hope this is the kind of response you were looking for! The project hasn't even happened yet, and I think you can consider yourself successful at kickstarting conversations about the role of social networking. If you have the time, I am eager to hear about what other types of responses you've gotten, and what this experience has been like for you so far. And I look forward to finding out what happens on the fateful days. :-)

Best,
David
(David was kept.)

Andrea:
I hope this message finds you doing well. I got your note about purge and just wanted to send you a quick note back. I think this is a very interesting and truly creative idea.

I only have 100 FB friends (which is small for facebook standards). Each one of my 100 friends, including you, I have known, been friends with and truly cared about at some point in my life. I use facebook as a way to see what these people whom I may have lost touch with, but haven't forgotten about as life progressed are up to. I only accept or ask for facebook friendships if I actually know the person and have spent time with them at some point in my life. I joined facebook fairly recently and at a point in my life when I needed the comfort of old friends, even if it be just through good memories. (my most fond memories of you are fun bus rides and days spent at Camp Givah!)

As the date of purge nears, I am going to put you on a limited profile. Due to what I explained above, I do not feel comfortable with strangers viewing my complete profile.

I wish you nothing but the best with this experiment and I hope you are doing well!! (Andrea was kept.)

Adrian:
Brian this is actually amazing. I AM PREPARED TO BE JUDGED! (Adrian was kept.)

Aparna:
happy purging, Brian!!! good luck with the shows – send me the show deets so that I can share with my london peeps...xoxo...

(Aparna was kept. She passed away in 2013, and this brief email exchange was the last we shared before her death.)

João:
OMG I'm scared! Remember it's always good to keep a Portuguese friend so that when Portugal sinks and disappears from the civilized-worth-being-talked-about-world you can sell me as a relic of a holy past long gone. Haaaaaaaaaa! How can I know when you'll be discussing our FB friendship? (I'm considering turning up in the moment with a bunch of flowers, a box of chocolates, and a paid holiday to the Maldives....all to convince your audience of my value...). (João did not bring flowers, chocolate, nor did he buy me a holiday to the Maldives... but he was kept.)

Renata:
Facebook is full of people who aggravate me daily. I put up with the narcissists who post a million aren't-i-so-beautiful photos, the morons who don't know how to spell, the look-how-happy-i-am married or engaged folks who post incessantly about their 'fiancee' or how they have the best hubby/wifey ever (gag), the people who give way too much information about their pregnancies or general health, the debbie downers, the people who drown us in photos of their kids, etc etc. And I do it because there are precious few people on there who I am genuinely thrilled to have reconnected with, to see how they're doing and to root on in life. And you are one of them. You make this social networking cluster-fuck worthwhile, and that is all you need to know. ...OK I'm done now. (Renata was kept.)

Additional Emails from *Purge*

Edu:
Looking forward to being purged! (Edu was purged. We have since re-friended.)

Joshua:
You appear to be binging on purge. (Joshua was kept.)

Emails received after *Purge*:

Carter (who had been deleted):
Hi Brian. I hope you are well. I honestly can't say that I'm surprised that I failed the test. When I saw the email saying that you were doing this, I was very tempted to reach out and tell you how cool I thought it was, but I kinda thought it might look like an attempt to "influence the judges."

It's funny how the very fact that you would do something like this is part of what makes me think you are someone worth knowing/being friends with. I realize you are probably overloaded with facebook contact at this point... so I'm not really expecting a reply. But I did want to say hi, and let you know how nifty I think this "project" was.

perhaps we could renew our relationship as "words with friends" opponents, even if we are not currently fb friends?

(We are currently Facebook friends.)

Maytal:
"she does stuff on youth and religion and she's not annoying to me" :)

i love it brian! I'm glad you kept me and i managed to tune in when you got to me.

This purge is quite addicting and I have to admit I was getting sorta nervous as my time came closer. It must be an exhausting process. You look awesome though and it seems like life is going really well. I'd love to hear about what your up to and if your heading back stateside for a visit anytime soon. I'd love to hear about your latest projects

Hope to hear from you soon,

Maytal

(We are currently Facebook friends.)

Melanie:

how sad I will miss you brian or you can feel free to re send me I would love to still be your friend

(We are currently Facebook friends.)

Mark:

Bye-bye.

(We are currently not Facebook friends.)

No email was sent to those friends who were kept.

purge

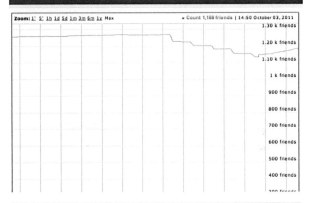

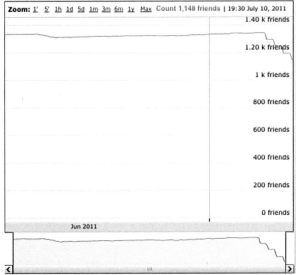

Charting real Facebook friend loss.
Graph and App designed by Chipp Jansen, 2011.

Purge Installation with Chrissie Dante
at EXIT Festival, Paris
Photo by Gregory Bohnenblust, 2013

Purge Installation with Amy Jephta
at Infecting The City, Cape Town
Photo by Sydelle Willow Smith, 2014

Q&As with *Purge* Installation Artists

The moment *Purge* finished on October 1st, 2011, I knew I could never do the installation again. My online community had been so supportive and engaged, but I also knew it was a legitimate stress on people's lives, and that it was quite unfair to ask my Facebook friends to keep being submitted through the process of *Purge* over and over again. And also, after two rounds, I felt like I had finally understood what a good, important Facebook friend looked like, and what a purge-able Facebook friend looked like. I now felt capable to do this big work all on my own, and in my own time.

As much fun as I think the one-hour stage show of *Purge* is, though, nothing is quite like having a raving artist talk about each of their Facebook friends for one minute. So everywhere I went (particularly in countries in which English is not the first language) I brought *Purge*, the installation, with a local artist going through their own list of friends for 6-24 hours. Working with each artist, they developed their own Introductory Email (explaining the project), Artistic Statement and Delete Email. The process I had engaged with to build *Purge* became the 'script' of the performance installation, and artists were free to act as auteurs, developing the work in a manner which made sense to them both artistically and personally.

As with my original performance installation, little documentation exists from these installations, but the impact was felt quite deeply by many. I asked each of the *Purge* artists to reflect on their own experience.

Alba von Von | Santarcangelo Festival Dei Teatri, 2014 | Translated by Michelle Davis

1) What was the reason you agreed to do *Purge*?

Ten months ago, I hid away from almost all my friends for many months. I was very ill, I didn't have enough energy to face other people. I wasn't me. I almost never answered my e-mails or phone, I avoided places where I knew I was bound to meet someone. I left my home only for very short periods of time.

I slowly recovered and reconnected with the ones I had pushed away. Some understand, some don't, but they are still very close to me. It's as if, almost without knowing it, I have real-life experienced the relational recovery of *Purge*.

2) How did you feel while performing *Purge*?

To Remove is a violent verb. Sometimes I felt ashamed to do it, because the people I wanted to eliminate were vague and pompous acquaintances, many involved in theatre...

Doing something others were forcing me to do made me feel very upset, as if I had to remove these people physically. It's hard for me to suspend judgment, to do something I don't completely believe in. But I did feel like a good attorney.

3) Have there been real-life consequences to performing the work?

Some people contacted me after being eliminated. Their tones were arrogant, humiliated. They didn't understand what the project was about – they just focused on their ego, as if my description actually undermined their true identity, their jobs, their relationships.

Some felt violated, all wanted to know how I had depicted them: Andy Warhol's five minutes of fame, they wanted to know more about themselves. Then they asked about the performance. It almost felt like a talent show where their success depended completely on me, on whether I said they were cool or not.

4) Would you perform it again?

Sure, I'd do it again ☺ It was really fun!

5) How have your opinions about technology or social networking changed or altered since before doing *Purge*?

I realised that for many the image they give away on Facebook – that sometimes does not correspond to reality – is very important. It has nothing to do with inventing, false names or storytelling: they use their real names, their photos, their way of being to build an online image that does not correspond to reality but allows you to show others what you decide to be, not your genuine self. I was and am not like that. I like to think of Facebook as a sort of potential collective narrative, a form which embraces both real and unreal information. Facebook is not reality but to some it counts for a lot: I observe social networks with growing detachment.

6) Is there anything else you'd like to say about the experience?

While the performance of *Purge* takes place, you slowly sink through the many levels of reality until for a short second you finally perceive it all.

Amy Jephta | Infecting the City, Cape Town, 2014

1) What was the reason you agreed to do *Purge*?

The concept intrigued me. It was also something I had been reflecting on personally for a while, so Brian's request came at a crucial moment. I'd been thinking about strategies to block out 'noise' in my life, especially the space taken up by people I didn't really care about.

2) How did you feel while performing *Purge*?

Anxious. It was really strange how doing something virtual and mostly intangible gave me sweaty palms in real life. Mostly I was worried about what my deleted friends would think. I hate having enemies and the thought that someone out there could feel antagonistic towards me as a result of this made me uneasy, to say the least. But once a few hours had passed, it became enormously liberating and almost (feel bad for saying this...) fun. The clicks stopped feeling so loaded.

3) Have there been real-life consequences to performing the work?

Yes. It weirdly continues to have ripple effects on my life. I received quite a few messages in the weeks and days following the performance. Some people wrote diplomatic notes about how they enjoyed being my friend, and were sorry to see me go. A few others re-requested me and said they were genuinely interested in my life, which was odd and honest. And then I had a few hostile responses – one person felt exploited, another had a rant against the nonsense I was calling 'art'. Now and then a person pops into my head, and I wonder what they've been doing. When I look them up on Facebook, I realise I haven't heard anything from them because they were Purged.

4) Would you perform it again?

Yes, highly likely. I wouldn't do it by myself, it implicates me too much. I liked the feeling of not being responsible. So I would do it, if it was in the same controlled environment with an audience etc.

5) How have your opinions about technology or social networking changed or altered since before doing *Purge*?

Well one thing I've followed through on, until today, is that I unfolllowed every single person on my Facebook. I'm friends with them, but my news feed is devoid of anything except recipe blogs (which I read to relax). It's brought a lot of calm to my life. I didn't have to break the automatic Facebook-checking habit, I still check the site about five times a day, but now there's nothing to see. It's made me realise that you need to carefully curate your digital life in the same way you curate your real life. I'd never willingly spend an evening in the company of people I find boring or have nothing in common with. Why then should I spend so many minutes a day actively giving those people my time?

It also means if there are people I *really* am interested in, I can search for them and see what they've been up to and talk to them. But it's purposeful, not automatic. This came about directly as a result of doing *Purge*.

Chrissie Dante | EXIT Festival, Maison des arts de Créteil (MAC), Paris, 2013 | Translated from French by Deborah Pearson

1) What was the reason you agreed to do *Purge*?

I found the project interesting. By accepting to 'purge' my Facebook 'friends', I was testing my own relationship to that resource, and I had to interrogate the ways that I use that resource (I have a pseudonym on Facebook, and I know very few of my eight hundred 'friends' in real life.) I also agreed to do the project because of the good rapport that Brian and I had since we first began corresponding on Skype. He's kind and has a good sense of humour.

2) How did you feel while performing *Purge*?

I felt a little stressed about the rules of the game, particularly the time limit. One minute to defend a friend (a friend who is, most likely, just virtual) is very short and that created a sense of frustration. I occasionally felt surprised by the ferocity of the 'jury' and the mercilessness that the game of the piece provoked in them. There was also a lot of laughter because by the end of four hours, my speech became much less considered, and I started talking about myself in relation to the people who were touched and personally implicated in the game.

3) Have there been real-life consequences to performing the work?

There weren't really direct consequences in my 'real' life, at least not in the long term. Some 'violent' reactions from 'friends' who had been cut by the jury took me by surprise a little.

4) Would you perform it again?

I mean, why not finish my Purge once I've started it? Yes.

5) How have your opinions about technology or social networking changed or altered since before doing *Purge*?

When preparing for *Purge*, I had to choose by eliminating from the game the Facebook pages of friends who weren't very interested in the performance. These 'friends' curiously ended up back on my newsfeed after I'd done the Purge. So because of that, I've actually felt a little less interested in going on Facebook lately.

6) Is there anything else you'd like to say about the experience?

The 'friends' who were difficult to defend were:

- People who use a photo of their kids as a profile picture.
- 'Friends' who I only really knew online (I actually had to lie a lot).
- 'Friends' who are also my idols!

Isabelle Bats | Fail Conference, Ghent, and Beurrschouwburg, Brussels, 2012-2013

1) What was the reason you agreed to do *Purge*?

I agreed to do *Purge* because I am a Facebook addict. Because I think it is right to question the notion of friendship, always.

2) How did you feel while performing *Purge*?

I felt like my energy was pumping me up even though I was getting more and more tired. I felt like my life was in my hands and people (the audience) somehow were getting me right!

3) Have there been real-life consequences to performing the work?

I think that four or five people might think that I am a total piece of shit as we speak but... no real life consequences so far.

4) Would you perform it again?

I would love to perform it again.

5) How have your opinions about technology or social networking changed or altered since before doing *Purge*?

My opinion about technology and social networking didn't change. I was already feeling the same way. *Purge* just has the finger on that pulse.

6) Is there anything else you'd like to say about the experience?

I loved meeting Brian. I loved having a nice glass of whiskey to soothe my throat. I loved having to be brainwashed a bit – it always helps.

Kymberlie Quong Charles | Fusebox Festival, Austin, 2015

1) What was the reason you agreed to do *Purge*?

For me there was not one particular reason to do *Purge*. I'd followed Brian's work on the piece since the very beginning, and I have so much love and appreciation for its spirit. I, too, think a lot about the role of social media in my life and what that means for my relationships 'IRL' and online. I think

Q&As with *Purge* Installation Artists

Purge is such a clever way to put a container around *some* of the questions that arise within Facebook relationships in a way that each role – performer, purge panel, audience, and the social network of the performer – are all invited to engage.

I'm also an emotional hoarder and deeply nostalgic. I saw the process of *Purge* as an opportunity to really examine lots of feelings, stories, dreams, that I've been holding onto for a long time and inquire whether they remain relevant to me. I found that I had maintained connections that were completely meaningless to me and therefore contributed to a big body of clutter and static which I'm constantly working to move out of my life. This fact actually made me a little uncomfortable, but realizing that I truly didn't care about my relationship with some of my Facebook 'friends' trumped my sense of being a good human being and making space for everyone.

Purge is also a little bit about relinquishing control, and giving other people a chance to let you know what they think of you. I know well that to be a whole person I/we all benefit from making ourselves vulnerable to feedback and powerlessness, but usually we are thrown unexpectedly into circumstances that target us in such ways. *Purge* lets us, the performer, invite feedback from our network and cede power to (often) total strangers about who will remain a 'friend.' It's humbling and scary but is very helpful for remaining grounded in the ideas that IT'S JUST ART (it really is), and THERE WAS LIFE BEFORE FACEBOOK... so just lean in.

Also, I was simply really excited to have a creative project, and to participate in a world, that of performance art, that I feel way outside of. I appreciated the thoughtful details Brian asks Purgers to complete in the lead up to the actual *Purge*. I knew that turning inward would feel important to me, but

I'd never experienced externalizing that process on a stage/livestream. It's a different way to compost your insides, and for me, somehow more meaningful or validating or affirming that the audience watching that process is invested in my story, filtered as it is, of my relationships.

2) How did you feel while performing *Purge*?

I mostly felt really joyful performing *Purge*. In the lead up to it I was scared that I would receive very negative feedback about my decision to participate and what that would mean for people in my network. As it turned out, I got very little negative feedback (and what I did receive was from people I probably would have purged anyway), and way more messages of love and affection than I anticipated. I remember a few moments of surprise finding that someone had pre-emptively purged me, but none that bothered me too much.

I felt a little self-conscious knowing I was on a livestream. I wondered whether my decisions would be judged, whether I looked pretty, whether my voice sounded too childish. At moments I wondered if I was being too caddy and just saying things to make it interesting, and at other times I felt really close to very earnest and authentic feelings about people in my life. Most of the latter are people for whom I have tremendous affection. I really liked being able to tell the world who was special to me.

3) Have there been real-life consequences to performing the work?

I can't think of any, although I wonder if there are people that I purged, or even that I didn't, that felt affected by getting cut or by something I might have said about them. It's always hard for me to learn that a friendship is more important to me than it is to the other person. That feels like a position I'm in often, but maybe I put others in that position, too, and then I broadcasted that to an international audience.

I ran into one of the people that pre-emptively purged me when I sent out the mass message about the project. I remember her response because she's someone that I generally liked, and I was surprised by her reaction. She wrote back and called it an 'icky, mean project' and I remember thinking, 'huh, she's not really the person I thought she was.' But when I ran into her she was just as sweet and friendly as ever. She wasn't harboring feelings about it I guess, meanwhile, I'd developed a judgement about her that I can't shake.

I did change a practice of mine following the performance. I've not thought a lot about exactly why, but since the *Purge* I started being more thoughtful about using Facebook's privacy tools to edit the type of access various people have to my content. I also started very liberally 'unfollowing' people (i.e. keeping them as friends but making their feeds invisible to me) rather than continuing to purge. I suppose these are other methods of purging that spare those I don't actually want much contact with the experience of being told they didn't make a cut.

4) Would you perform it again?

In a heartbeat.

5) How have your opinions about technology or social networking changed or altered since before doing *Purge*?

I take a nosedive into some big existential questions with this prompt. I'm not sure that my opinions about technology and social networking have changed, per se. I suppose I'm in a camp of people that views technology and social working as a fact of our present and future, and so the questions for me are how do we we use these for good, in ways that enhance lives, and not in ways that make people less physically or emotionally safe. And I also worry about the disembodied nature of online relationships of all sorts, and what that will mean for our emotional intelligence down the evolutionary road. I feel pretty sure that unless there are mindful interventions along the way, we will move farther and farther from a spiritual and emotional sense of ourselves, which is, in my opinion, a tragedy of humanity.

6) Is there anything else you'd like to say about the experience?

It was such an honor to take part in *Purge*. I wish everyone I knew had the privilege of being able to pause and interrogate their engagement with their relational world. I found it to be a satisfying emotional exercise that left me feeling more connected to myself above anything.

Purge Installation with Jeff Mills
at Fusebox Festival, Austin
Photo by Cami Alys, 2015

The *Purge*

(The names have been changed to protect the innocent)

Blog Post by Jeff Mills, April 2015.

**Commissioned by Fusebox Festival
and edited by Timothy Braun
Reprinted with permission**

For what it's worth I found the entire thing (at least the way it was handled) to be self-centered, childish, and offensive. No, you did not have my permission to involve me in your 'art.' Subjects and/or participants should always be informed and willing, or at the bare minimum warned. I was none of these things.

Though I have no idea to what extent I was put on display (though I heard there was a live feed which leads me to believe it was not small) I'd imagine there was, at least to some degree, a violation of my privacy by way of displaying my profile to strangers. This isn't clever, or cute, or funny, it's a violation of trust.

Additionally there was the attempt to distance yourself from the choice via the email. To me it came off as a disclaimer of responsibility for the entire stunt. If you had removed me from your friends list, I would have understood. People have their reasons. We don't speak much. We're not close. Mostly we're acquaintances by way of Jim. I get that. I would hold no ill will towards you. Indeed, you've little reason to keep me. However, that's a decision a responsible adult makes and then stands by it. One doesn't pass the buck. Doing so shows not only the lack of friendship (which again is easily understandable), but a lack of respect – something I'm confident I'd never experience from Jim or Mandy and I would have thought I wouldn't have to put up with from their friends.

I caution you to seriously reconsider this stunt as art. You violated trust, privacy, and friendships. You attempted to pass what should have been your responsibility to a group of strangers. You involved people against their will. Unknowingly, yes, but how could you have known since you didn't ask. So while maybe you were trying to learn something about yourself you failed to give a shit about other people entirely. I hope the experience was worth something to you because in my mind it cost you a lot.

Furthermore, I'd like you to look again at what I wrote above. I did not say the stunt was offensive, or wrong, merely the way in which you handled it. I'm all for social experimentation, but have some ethics. Were I you I'd un-friend that artist friend of yours. But hey, I don't know the person. So who am I to judge –Jeremy

For 12 hours, over the course of two days, I sat in a coffee shop in Austin, TX and let anyone who was interested sit on a panel of three judges while I defended my Facebook friendships to them in alphabetical order. I was given one minute to defend each relationship to the panel. After the allotted time, a buzzer would sound and the jury was forced to make a decision: keep or delete. If they chose to keep, nothing happened, if they chose to delete I 'de-friended' that person on the spot and sent them a pre-written form letter explaining the situation. Each of my Facebook friends received an invitation to the event prior to its beginning, explaining their involvement, and they were given an opportunity to opt-out or delete me pre-emptively. (Although, let's face it, not everyone opens their Facebook event invitations, especially from someone you have not heard from in 20 years.) There was a live feed of the event broadcast to all of my Facebook friends allowing them to watch this process in real-time. This concoction was the brainchild of London-based artist Brian Lobel.

Initially, this project piqued my interest as a way to examine my own relationships with people as well as my own, perhaps subconscious, relationship with the medium of Facebook. The questions seemed simple enough: What does Facebook friendship mean? How does this piece of technology change my perspective on friendship? What lines are blurred? Am I becoming complacent in my 'real world' relationships? Does being digital friends dilute the quality of my friendship? This, however, was just the surface level of the questions to come. As the days before the installation approached, I began getting reactions to my announcement that I was participating in *Purge* from many of my Facebook friends. The reactions were wide and varied, and from people in every nook and corner of my life. People consider Facebook differently. For some it was offensive, for some exciting, for others a real violation of their own privacy (even though Facebook is essentially a public forum) and for many a very dangerous act that I was embarking on. My new round of questions definitely cut deeper. Where will this danger come from? How will people perceive my perception of them? Why do people immediately assume they will be purged? Will I view the audience as adversaries? Are real friendships on the line?

> *Your email made me think of various things given that I recently turned 35. I thought about how we aren't friends and never were while we were in high school. It made me a bit sad because I can't help but wonder if our prejudices in high school kept us from learning from each other in this adult life .. Now... But it is what it is. Given that we are no longer going*

*to be FB friends, I wanted to share my best memory
of you. I wore your ex' same perfume .. And you
took it in and told me how it reminded you of her.
I could tell how that took you to a far away place that
only the two of you knew. I remember wondering
what that was as you looked off. We were in the
courtyard. I remember thinking that you loved her
more than she loved you. For a moment I felt like I
knew you. —Christina*

Purge is the wrong word for my experience. I learned I want more friends, not less.

At its best, *Purge* is a fascinating examination of our modern culture and the human experience. An exercise in memory recall, stamina and articulation. At its worst, it feels like bullying. A public shaming. An invasion of someone else's privacy and trust.

Is anyone objective when considering someone else's relationships?

Why close off an opportunity for future interaction with someone? Why bring the public to judge our relationships in a game show style? These are real people. It was like cutting a birthday cake with a chainsaw. Why bully? Why judge? Ego. Both mine and the jury's.

Facebook is subjective, but to me it is a coward's act to not engage with someone face-to-face if you want something different from them. We have no hope that through compassion, empathy, and communication we cannot salvage or re-invigorate a relationship. True, people take emotional space in our lives, but friendship is not a garage sale, an old worn chair does not have feelings about being kicked to the curb.

I felt at times the people from my past were dehumanized. I don't like their cover photo. De-friend. Too many dog pictures. De-friend. You mispronounced their name. De-friend. Everyone has value to me. I would prefer to keep the unknown possibility of someone's potential friendship as a future opportunity, not a 'what have they done for me lately' dismissal. Let's keep the doors to friendship open, not close them. I don't believe we have enough friends. Engage each other, don't run, and if someone is really a poison then say good-bye to them, humanely.

I truly enjoyed taking time out of my normal routine to stop and consider all the people from my life. I rarely do 300 in a row over the course of six hours, but it's beautiful to consider someone. I remembered their voice, the places we had been, the times, the meals, the hairstyles, their laugh, the plays we did together, the smell of perfume from a girl that didn't love me as much I loved her.

I have never felt more loved from such a wide audience. People sent me sweet memories. The process solidified my hypothesis that I am a lover. I love 'hard' and am thankful for everyone I have had in my life, warts and all. I am grateful to Brian Lobel for this opportunity. How often does one get tasked with defending everyone in their life? I'm not talking about your best friends or family, but the ones you haven't seen in 20 years, that friend who cooked you pasta, the guy who worked for that festival who brought you food, your girlfriend from second grade. My girlfriend in the second grade was my first girlfriend. Her name is Becky. She was cut by the *Purge* jury.

> There are those who lives you affected, change the direction of their course. Many times you don't even know it. You had that effect on me. Purge or not, you had and still have a profound effect on the way I lead my life. I've told you before...thanks Jeff.
> –Mike

In the same way it is difficult to articulate the full scope of impact of someone in your life in 60 seconds, it is difficult to articulate the comprehensive impact of *Purge* in a blog post.

I will sit with it for years to come. Let's talk about it. When I see you. In real time.

Performing in *Purge* is like going to your own funeral, having a unique chance to tell everyone you have ever had a connection with what they meant to you. Facebook friends are perhaps like books, just because I have not read that book on World War II motorcycles recently, or perhaps at all, doesn't mean I won't want to read it in 15 years. I got the book for a reason. I suppose the 'counter' argument to that is that your bookshelf is only so large, and can only contain so many books, but I would argue to get another book shelf if you can, more books is more books. One day you might go to the shelf and the shelf is empty.

Weirdo. –Jamie

'Delete' Email by *Purge* artist
Kymberlie Quong Charles[13]

Dear (former) Facebook friend,

Remember that message I sent you about PURGE and how I was going to let three random people decide the fate of our Facebook friendship? Well, you ended up on the cut list. I had 60 seconds to defend our friendship; I did my best.

This estrangement may be of no consequence to you at all, or you may be devastated. If the latter is the case, I'm truly sorry. Luckily, in the world of digital friendships, we all have a lot of agency. Here are some options:

1) The result of the PURGE could remain permanent and we don't ever have to speak again.

2) You could reFacebookfriend me again and it will be as if nothing ever happened, if we choose to pretend nothing ever happened.

3) We could transition our friendship to something that does not entail a Facebook relationship. I actually have many true friends who are not on Facebook at all. We find different ways to relate. I probably just see fewer photos of their lives.

In any case, I'd like to think that at some point in the course of social media connection we've contributed to each other's lives in some way. I hope you feel similarly, regardless of how you choose to proceed.

Warmly,

Kymberlie

---

[13] Kymberlie's adapted DELETE email is a great example of how to take *Purge* and make a process meaningful to yourself. Go ahead and do the *Purge* your own way: You'll feel better, then worse, then better. Promise.

Photo by Christa Holka

Brian Lobel is a performer, teacher and curator who is interested in creating work about bodies and how they are watched, policed, poked, prodded and loved by others. The New York-born, London-based performer has shown work internationally in a range of contexts, from the Sydney Opera House, to Harvard Medical School, to Lagos Theatre Festival, and [hundreds of] galleries, hospitals, cabarets, forests and museums in between, blending provocative humor with insightful reflection.

WWW.OBERONBOOKS.COM

Follow us on www.twitter.com/@oberonbooks
& www.facebook.com/OberonBooksLondon